© Vinciane Verguethen

ALINA SIMONE

YOU MUST GO AND WIN

Alina Simone is a critically acclaimed singer who was born in Kharkov, Ukraine, and now lives in Brooklyn. Her music has been covered in a wide range of media, including the BBC's *The World*, NPR, *Spin*, *Billboard*, *The New Yorker*, and *The Wall Street Journal*. This is her first book. For more information about Simone, visit www.alinasimone.com.

YOU MUST GO AND WIN

YOU MUST GO AND WIN

ALINA SIMONE

FABER AND FABER, INC.
AN AFFILIATE OF FARRAR, STRAUS AND GIROUX
NEW YORK

Faber and Faber, Inc.
An affiliate of Farrar, Straus and Giroux
18 West 18th Street, New York 10011

Copyright © 2011 by Alina Simone
Distributed in Canada by D&M Publishers, Inc.
Printed in the United States of America
First edition, 2011

Illustration on pages 66–67 by Ben Coonley. Illustrations on pages 111–18 by Vladimir Zimakov.

Library of Congress Cataloging-in-Publication Data
Simone, Alina, 1974–
    You must go and win / Alina Simone.— 1st ed.
        p.   cm.
    ISBN 978-0-86547-915-9 (alk. paper)
    1. Simone, Alina, 1974–   2. Alternative rock musicians—United States—
Biography.   I. Title.

ML420.S5634A3 2011
782.42166092—dc22
[B]
                                                        2010022649

Designed by Jonathan D. Lippincott

www.fsgbooks.com

10 9 8 7 6 5 4 3 2 1

*For Josh: I couldn't love you more
if Jesus flew out of your mouth*

CONTENTS

YOU MUST GO AND WIN

THE KOMSOMOL TRUTH

n late September 2008, I received an email from one ELMON-STRO with the subject line "Hello, Alina! Kharkov on the Line!" ELMONSTRO's real name, it turned out, was Kiril, and he was a journalist for the Kharkov bureau of the newspaper *Komsomolskaya Pravda*, which he translated for me as "Komsomol True." He had learned that I was born in Kharkov and wanted to interview me about my new album, a collection of songs covering the Soviet punk singer Yanka Dyagileva. "If will please you," Kiril wrote, "reveal to us all news about your creation."

It was the first time that anyone from the Ukrainian city where I was born had ever taken an interest in my music, and I was surprised. A little touched, even. My family had left the Soviet Union as political refugees when I was too young to remember, but sometimes I felt it anyway: a Kharkov-shaped hole in my heart. Not to mention that the motherland had come calling when I was feeling particularly homeless, having just moved from North Carolina to a temporary sublet in Brooklyn. My new apartment occupied the top floor of an old brownstone that was badly in need of repair. The closet doors were lying in a heap on the floor when I arrived, and there were holes the size of hand grenades beneath the rotted windowsills. Spinning the hot water tap in the shower felt like placing an outside bet on a roulette wheel. And the water didn't emerge from the showerhead so much as the wall, like it was some kind of life-giving rock. I would press myself against the runoff in the mornings, before the tiles could suck away what little remained of its warmth. It was the kind of place that made you think too much about your station in life, your dimming prospects. If nothing else, I figured, an interview with "Komsomol True" could serve as a pleasant distraction from speed-dialing the three phone numbers my landlady had given me for her possibly imaginary handyman.

We left Kharkov because my father was blacklisted by the KGB, but whenever I asked why, Papa always replied that he'd never know for sure. Did I think he just received a form letter in the mail one day on KGB stationery that began "We regret to inform you . . ." and ended with a neat summary of his transgressions? If provoked further, he'd always end up demurring, "Don't make me out to be some kind of dissident freedom fighter," then retreat to a yellow legal pad full of equations. He refused to romanticize our flight from the Soviet Union, to let me imagine it as some kind of action-adventure movie from the eighties. *It's not like I ever slayed a Stormtrooper*, his warning glance seemed to say, *or breakdanced my way to freedom*.

Papa did admit, however, that it probably had something to do with turning the KGB down when they made him a recruitment offer in college. In any case, it was soon afterward that bad things insisted on happening to my family. My father's military health exemption (he'd had polio as a child) was revoked without warning and instead of serving in the officer corps, like most college graduates, he was sent off to work in the notoriously brutal building brigades of the Soviet army, alongside violent criminals. My mother was forced to quit her job and was mysteriously unable to find work, despite graduating with top honors from the state university. Unemployment was officially illegal, but she stayed home with me in the flat we shared with my father's parents and sister while Papa drifted through a string of menial jobs, rarely lasting long at any of them.

You wouldn't know it from looking at my family now, though. Within two years of leaving the Soviet Union, my father had his PhD in physics and a job at a good university. My mother, like most Russian immigrants, found work doing something with computers that I didn't understand. And despite having just completed a thoroughly money-losing tour of the United States, even I had distinguished myself enough as a singer to merit an interview request from a newspaper in Kharkov. Thinking that this called for a self-congratulatory moment, I forwarded the message to my parents. I didn't bother including a note, but the subtext was clear.

From my parents—usually quick with the email—there was a suspicious silence. A few hours later, my phone rang.

"I had no idea that rag still existed," my mother said as soon as I picked up the phone. "You realize that was the official Communist newspaper?"

I knew that Komsomol was the abbreviated name for the youth division of the Communist Party and had to admit that it did sound pretty retro. But I was still willing to give Kiril the benefit of the doubt.

"Well, it's a brand, after all—maybe they just didn't want to give up on a solid brand after investing so much in it during Soviet times?"

"Are you seriously considering doing this interview?"

I hadn't even considered not considering it. And why did Mama always have to act like someone just dropped an ice cube down her pants?

"Of course," I answered.

And then my mother gave a very Russian kind of snort that could roughly be translated as "This is unbelievable and you are an idiot," and hung up the phone.

For the rest of the day, I waited for some word from my father, but finally overcome with impatience, I decided to give him a call, just to make sure he'd gotten the message. When I reached him, he sounded a little surprised.

"What email?"

"From Kharkov! The one from *Komsomolskaya Pravda*."

"Mmm. I think I remember something about that."

"And?"

"Well," my father said, with a tiny chuckle, "I guess it is *interesting*." He seemed to draw some amusement from the situation, albeit from a very great distance, as though something mildly droll had just happened to an acquaintance on a planet in a parallel universe.

I wrote back to Kiril that night and explained that I would love to do the interview, but since I couldn't write in Russian, it would be best if he just sent me the questions in Russian and I responded in English. But somehow I did a bad job communicating this request, because from that day forward, Kiril wrote to me in a dialect of English that might best be described as Google Translate on Acid.

Hello, Alina. I was pleasantly surprised, when got a rapid answer from you. Very interestingly me with you to communicate. Our musicians stick to very with self-confidence and journalists are not loved. I am a rad, that you are quite another man. If you will not object—I prepared questions by which I and our readers able to know you better. Here list of questions:

Though feeling a bit damaged by the Tilt-a-Whirl quality of Kiril's prose, I moved on to the questions themselves and found that they fell into exactly three equally irritating categories.

The first category consisted of questions that I couldn't understand at all. At the top of this list was "Do you have any zoons?" I had no idea what a zoon was. Having spent much of the past eight years surrounded by indie-rock guys whose favorite intimidation tactic always began "You've seriously never heard of [insert name of yesterminute's most popular band here]?," the zoon threw me into a small panic. I was convinced it was some really cool Ukrainian thing, the measure by which my own coolness would be judged. It was bad enough worrying about my relative coolness in one country without exposing myself to the judgment of zoon-loving Ukrainian hipsters. I didn't think that I had any, but regardless, decided it was safer to politely ignore this one.

The second category consisted of questions that I technically could answer, but very much preferred not to. This list included questions like: Are you very beautiful? Did not you think about the career of movie actor? Why exactly fate, considered that it is not quite womanish employment? Do you like to cook? Who you on the sign of zodiac? Did not you have a desire to engage in physics? Do you watch after that takes place now in Ukraine? Do you want to arrive to Kharkov with concerts?

The last category of questions, I had to admit, were best answered by my parents themselves. These included: Where lived? Where walked in child's garden, in school? In what age you were driven away from Kharkov? What now do your parents get busy?

"I hope on a collaboration," Kiril wrote before signing off with his regards, "and will be with impatience!"

Although my parents clearly were refusing to drink the Kool-Aid, I decided to forward the questions to them anyway, pointing out which ones they might answer if they had the time. Minutes later I received the following response from my mother:

> Alina,
> Could you please stop this "collaboration" for God's sake! I cannot read this nonsense anymore!
> This is pure delirium.
> m.

My father's one-line response was:

> I like "I am a rad" in Kiril's message.

And that was it. Neither of them answered the questions or so much as implied that they would. But the next day, there was a message from my mother with an attachment labeled "Early Childhood" and a note that said:

> Alina,
> Here is a template for all inquiries of this kind. You should keep it for the future and use "cut & paste" for the next idiot from "Komsomol True."
> m.

Then, despite Mama's professed ambivalence about my interview, I received another message from her within twenty minutes, when I failed to respond instantaneously to the first one:

> Is this all? That much for your feedback!
> In any case please don't forget to bring the kitchen knives for me. Please put them in your luggage right now.
> m.

I opened the attachment and found that my mother had conveniently decided to write her history of my early childhood from my first-person perspective:

I left Kharkov at the age of one year. To preschool I never did go. This was unnecessary because my mother was forced to take leave of her job "by her own volition" (or rather, that of her supervisor). In this fashion, she was able to stay at home with me.

My father was a night watchman. He guarded the kiosk next to the concert hall Ukraina in Shevchenko Park. The kiosk was called Café Lira. Port wine was sold there and candies as well (probably as a snack for after drinking port wine). Besides this, there was nothing else to guard in the kiosk. Papa was given a job there with the hope that he would drink less than the other watchmen. And this hope was fully realized.

One day my papa had a stroke of good fortune—he was offered a job moonlighting as a night watchman at the zoo, which was located nearby. In this fashion, he could guard two locations simultaneously. But this happiness was short lived—he lasted only a month and a half before someone filed an anonymous report against him, revealing that he had a higher education. The director of the zoo did not want any trouble and Papa was fired.

From time to time, my parents were summoned by the KGB for "a chat." There they were given the never-changing, standard question: "What is the real reason that you are leaving the country?" To which they would give the standard response: "To reunite with our relatives," and then something about the humane policies of the Party and the government. After these fruitful ex-

changes they were usually told, "Wait, we will notify you."
And then everything would repeat itself.

My mother had cleverly avoided answering any of the questions I had highlighted and was clearly presenting a version of events *Komsomolskaya Pravda* was unlikely to deem publishable. So I cheerfully forwarded it on, sending the whole thing off to ELMONSTRO unedited. With my parents' questions out of the way, it was time to focus on my own. I considered just doing a rush job. (*Are you very beautiful?* Yes. *Do you have any zoons?* No.) But I ended up dutifully responding to each question in turn. Slowly the fascinating portrait of a Libra with no interest in acting and no aptitude for physics, who could be said to like cooking only if making coffee counts, began to emerge.

The last question was the most difficult: *Do you want to arrive to Kharkov with concerts?* I had talked to enough newspapers in the various places I'd called home over the past few years to know the kind of local boosterism required of me here, but I could not seem to fluff myself up to the task. I considered trying to explain, but what kind of pixelated meaning would emerge from Kiril's random word generator when he learned that the only relative my family stayed in touch with back in Kharkov was a man known to me as the Cousin Who Drinks Water? I hesitated to put it in cold print, but the truth was that I didn't want to arrive in Kharkov with concerts; I had already gone back once and found there just wasn't much to return to.

It was my grandfather's death that convinced me to go back. A geography professor and decorated World War II veteran, my grandfather was an unflinching Kharkov patriot. Throughout my childhood, he sent us postcards with photographs of impossibly boring buildings born of some hideous concrete wafflemaker that said things like "Kharkov, My City, My Motherland." He kept sending them even after the economy collapsed, the city shut all the streetlamps off at night, and he was forced to provide the bed sheets, gauze, and syringes for his own prostate surgery. I figured there would always be time to go see him. At eighty-six, my grandfather was still quite spry. It was that way right up until the night he went to sleep and never woke up. I was surprised to be shaken by his death, considering this was a man I had never known, a black-and-white photograph labeled "Dedushka." But I was, and I blamed my own inertia for not visiting him in Ukraine or even just picking up the phone to say hello. I had a lot of excuses for not calling. Mostly I was worried there'd be nothing to talk about. But there was also the very real danger that my aunt Lyuda would pick up the phone. And what could I possibly say to a woman whose last letter to my father had announced, "If I could strangle you with my own hands, I would"?

All families are complicated. Those forced to live according to the whims of a totalitarian regime perhaps more so. And those, like mine, where some members of the family flee, leaving the remaining members exposed to unhelpful levels of KGB scrutiny, can be described as completely fucked. The day my parents filed their application to leave the Soviet Union, both of my mother's parents were forced to resign from their jobs at the pharmaceutical research institutes where they had worked for over twenty-five years. By way of explanation they were posed the following rhetorical question: "How can you be expected to produce good research when you can't even discipline your own child?" A few years later they joined us in Massachusetts. My father's family, on the other hand, was left more or less unmolested; Papa's parents both managed to keep their jobs and seemed to live contentedly enough. But soon bad news began drifting over to us from Ukraine, in letters written on painfully translucent paper and via phone calls from my father's cousin. A year after we emigrated, my grandfather was forced to retire from his job. Then, in the post-Perestroika years, the family suffered a series of financial setbacks followed by my grandmother's sudden death from diabetes. Aunt Lyuda blamed Papa's flight from the Soviet Union for putting them all in peril, and for all of the family's current problems besides. So they no longer spoke to each other, and Mama, who already used the word *idiot* as if it were a common pronoun, especially had nothing nice to say about that side of the family.

But family matters aside, Kharkov lacked other kinds of appeal. It didn't cast a particularly long shadow over world history like the ancient capital of Kiev. Nor was it a beautiful jewel-box city like Lvov. Invariably, the two words people used to describe Kharkov were either *industrial* or *big*. Occasionally *big* and *industrial* were helpfully combined to yield the illuminating phrase "a big industrial city." I grew up in a sleepy colonial town west of Boston and had very little experience with big industrial cities. So I pictured Kharkov as an apocalyptic version of Springfield or Worcester, places we drove through from time to time on our way to somewhere more picturesque. And I had to admit, traveling five thousand miles just to visit the Worcester of Ukraine wasn't the most enticing proposition.

After my grandfather died, the only member of the family who Papa stayed in touch with was the Cousin Who Drinks Water. This was the nickname we gave my father's cousin Lyonya after he sent Papa a twelve-page letter which began with the question "What is Health?" The answer, it turned out, was water. In particular, salt water. And the letter went on to detail the many benefits of drinking salt water in various unorthodox ways, culminating in the optimally beneficial process of drawing it up through your nose. Lyonya was a loyal proponent of this system and vigorously recommended Papa adopt it for himself. The only drawback, he explained, is that sometimes a loose bit of water might fall out of your face during the course of conversation. A small enough price to pay for immortality.

Papa was greatly amused by the letter and felt the urge to share it with someone, but when it came to letters from Kharkov, Mama was never in a sharing mood. So he called me into his study instead and read it out loud, which is how Lyonya became the Cousin Who Drinks Water. It was a long nickname to be sure, a bit awkward in the mouth, but Papa and I were committed to it. The only other story I ever remembered hearing about Lyonya was after my parents' sole return to the former Soviet Union in 1990. I asked Papa how it was seeing his cousin again for the first time in almost fifteen years, and Papa replied, "It was great. He stood on his head for us."

Now, I knew that Papa was very fond of Lyonya, who had supported him through many difficult times back in Kharkov and dutifully passed on the American dollars he sent every month to cover my grandfather's living expenses. The rather fanciful image of his cousin Papa conjured for me can probably be chalked up to the fact that I was a child at the time. Perhaps he also wanted to somehow lighten my impression of life in Kharkov, which only seemed to run the short gamut from crappy to unbearable. In any case, despite my warped image of the Cousin Who Drinks Water, after my grandfather died, Lyonya was the only person left who could show me the things I wanted to see in Kharkov. And it suddenly occurred to me that he wasn't getting any younger either.

When I announced that I was planning to visit Kharkov, my normally absentminded father snapped to attention. The first thing he said was "That's a bad idea," followed quickly by "Do me a favor and don't tell Mama."

But Mama did not react as badly as we thought she would. "Great!" she yelled, launching into full-throated someone-is-shoving-an-ice-cube-down-my-pants mode. "Now maybe you will finally know what a godforsaken hole we rescued you from!" Mama assured me that I would return from Ukraine and spend the rest of my days showering her with things she liked: marzipan molded into animal shapes, gift certificates to Loehmann's, et cetera.

For weeks Papa kept trying to dissuade me from going, but when I held firm and even managed to convince Josh, my long-suffering husband, to come along, he grudgingly arranged for a meeting with the Cousin Who Drinks Water. Then, shortly before we left, Papa also coughed up the following unenthusiastic summary of Places of Family Importance in Kharkov:

The most important place is the house where we lived. The address is Krasnoshkol'naya Naberezhnaya 26, apt. 96. It stands near a rather stinky river called Lopan. You are welcome to take a walk along the bank.

The next destination is Kharkov State University. This is in a very big square. In the middle of the square is a park named after Dzerzhinsky—the founder of the KGB. I skipped many classes reading physics books in this park.

Right next to the university is a park called Sad Shevchenko. The marble statue of Shevchenko (a famous Ukrainian poet) is kind of OK. I studied in this park as well.

From Sad Shevchenko you can get to the zoo and see the sad animals. I had a brief career as a night watchman in the zoo, and a more lasting one guarding a small kiosk in the zoo, called Café Petushok.

And just to make sure I hadn't somehow missed his point, Papa added a final note: "Even if this sounds like fun, I suspect it won't be."

Josh and I arrived by train from Kiev on the Stolichniy Express, seated on a bench of genuine Soviet pleather, nervously squeezing hands when we felt the final jolt signaling our arrival. Then an attendant lowered a metal ladder to the platform, and we stepped down, feet finally firm on warm Kharkov concrete. Blinking back nonexistent tears, I stood there uncertainly, waited for the rush of feeling. But there was nothing. Nothing but this sense of whistling disorientation. Making our way to the station, I stopped to examine the Kharkov city emblem prominently mounted to the wall. It featured wreaths of wheat, bushels of fruit, and, hovering above them both, the symbol for nuclear energy. Radiation and produce, I thought to myself, a combination that screamed an urgent need for rebranding. Once inside, we found the station itself unexpectedly sumptuous. From the soaring ceilings and massive chandeliers, one would think we'd just pulled in to one of the loftier cities of Europe. There was no trace of the cold boot of Soviet oppression. If only my family had lived in the train station, we could have been happy here.

The first practical order of business was to inform my parents we hadn't been vaporized at the border. Conveniently, we found an internet kiosk right inside the station. The cramped room had three computers lined up against one wall and was presided over by a bulbous woman stuffed behind a desk.

"Can I buy fifteen minutes of internet time?" I asked in Russian.

The woman gave me a sour look. I found myself unable to tear my eyes away from her halo of pinkish-burgundy hair. It looked like one of those fiber-optic lamps you see in the windows of head shops, and I half expected it to start rotating.

"Internet? What internet?" she barked.

I apologized for mistaking her for someone who might help us and we went next door to see if the lady at the dry-cleaning kiosk knew where to find whoever was in charge.

"Wait a minute," said the dry-cleaning lady, and tore open the side door separating the two rooms.

"Sveta!" she yelled. "For God's sake, you can't just pretend you don't work here whenever the tourists come around."

Confused by the torrent of Russian, Josh turned to me.

"What was that?"

"She was pretending she didn't work here."

"Oh," Josh said. "I'm going to go find a bathroom."

I was still working on the email when Josh wandered back into the room.

"No one will tell me where the bathroom is."

"Maybe they can't understand English?"

"It's weird," he said, "I think they understand me fine. They just didn't want to tell me where it is."

So we went off in search of the men's room, and it turned out to be a good thing because I'd forgotten that the ladies' room would only be marked by an inscrutable Cyrillic letter that looks like nothing so much as a caterpillar trying its best to run away from you.

We had booked a room at the Hotel Kharkov because, in my parents' day, it had been the grandest hotel in the city. And clearly it *had* once been grand. The richly columned interior looked as though the Sistine Chapel had thrown up on it. Unlike the train station, though, the Hotel Kharkov was also alarmingly run-down. As I struggled to find a camera angle that didn't include child-sized holes in the wall, gaping wires, or what I could have sworn were traces of bullet-strafing, I detected an unmistakable whiff of downtown Beirut to the place. On the way to our room, we found that an army unit had been stationed down the hall from us. The wiry young men, all naked from the waist up, regarded us suspiciously as we made our way past them, their eyes glinting like hard candy.

As soon as we closed the door behind us, Josh went over to one of the cot-sized beds and lay down, face-first.

"Do me a favor?" he said, voice muffled. "Don't go out there."

I took a photo of him lying there, then walked over to the window and pulled back the curtain. There, in vivid green and gray, were the Soviet postcards of my youth. The hotel overlooked Freedom Square, which was supposedly the largest square in Europe, second in size worldwide only to China's Tiananmen Square. As Papa mentioned, it used to be called Dzerzhinsky Square, and perhaps for that reason, its new name still managed to sound ominous. The western end was completely dominated by a statue of Lenin that looked to be about three stories high. And although most of the vast cobblestoned expanse was empty, the grassy stretch surrounding Lenin was teeming with students. They sat in colorful clumps on each of the four tiers that made up the base of his pedestal. Lenin himself was dressed in a business suit, tie tucked into vest, with a rather stylish coat rakishly thrown across his shoulders. In his left hand he held what appeared to be a rolled-up newspaper or an umbrella, but was probably something far more symbolic, like a small, frightened farmer. His right hand was raised, outstretched toward the square in a gesture meant to say, "Come, Comrades, join me in building a glorious future!" but which today looked a little more Vanna White–ish. "Welcome, Comrades, to Europe's biggest parking lot!"

We had agreed to meet the Cousin Who Drinks Water for our tour of Important Family Places in front of the hotel at three, and so we went outside to wait. Ten minutes later, a lonely figure emerged, trekking toward us across the endless slab of freedom.

At first sight, I had to admit I was a little disappointed. Cousin Lyonya was a balding, slightly paunchy guy with soft features. He wore beachy knee-length shorts and a black t-shirt that said "Yacht Club," and could easily have been mistaken for a customer-service representative from Hertz Rent-a-Car. He didn't look much like Papa at all. Nor did he resemble Popeye the Sailor or some other quirky superhero who might thrive on salt water alone. It had been my secret hope that at some point during the afternoon, we might slip away to some shady spot where Cousin Lyonya would stand on his head for us. This hope was quietly dashed. Trying not to sound despondent, I asked Lyonya if he was still drinking water. But at this he only shook his head and laughed.

The suggestion to visit Dedushka's grave was waved away as too complicated, so instead we struck off on the scenic route toward our first destination, Krasnoshkol'naya Naberezhnaya 26, the apartment building where my family once lived. It was a beautiful July day and downtown Kharkov's dignified prerevolutionary buildings were lit up like pastel flares in the sun. We had just settled into a pleasant amble, crossing the square and turning down a wide, leafy boulevard, when Lyonya turned to me and asked, "So why don't you have any children?"

Even though we had known each other for all of eight minutes, I wasn't surprised by the question, having grown up fending off the invasive inquiries of ruthlessly blunt Russians. I still remembered being greeted at the door by my parents' friends one Thanksgiving with the exclamation "But you are so much greasier than last year!"

"How old are you anyway?" Lyonya continued. "You must be at least thirty by now."

"We're planning on having kids," I said, feeling like Jennifer Aniston. "We just haven't gotten around to it yet." I looked nervously at Josh, who was enjoying the view of the park.

"Because a woman should have children while she is still young and healthy. Like here in Kharkov. Our women give birth when they are twenty or twenty-two years old. *This* is considered normal." He shot me a look from the corner of his eye as if to underscore what was not considered normal.

"But maybe that is because our women are so irresistible," Lyonya went on. "Like that one there, eh, Joshua?" He raised his eyebrows at a passing blonde. "Wouldn't you say she is very luscious?"

"What's he saying?" Josh asked, suddenly with us again.

"Oh, you know." I shrugged, taking his hand. "Just Welcome-to-Kharkov stuff."

For the rest of our walk, our attention was focused on the various landmarks. "Here, on the left, you will notice the Monument to a Soldier-Defender of the City of Kharkov, built to commemorate Soviet victory in the Great Patriotic War," Cousin Lyonya would say. And I would lamely circle the statue with a camera while Lyonya called after me, "Try it from the other side. Get the sun behind you. Don't forget the inscription!" Nothing, I soon discovered, sucked the fun out of history like a ginormous statue of a guy pointing a gun at the sky. It was a relief when we finally crossed the Lopan River and stopped before a nondescript brick building partly obscured by a billboard for Zlatagor Vodka.

"Here it is," Lyonya announced. "Your old home."

Most people, when taken to the doorway of a typical Soviet-era apartment building, think they've mistakenly arrived at the service entrance. They find a series of crumbling steps, a pair of doors that form a kind of sheet-metal sandwich, and a grim facade of concrete or dirty brick punctuated by the occasional disintegrating balcony. Our apartment building was no different from the rest. The only strange thing was that throughout my life, everyone in my family had always insisted that the flat in Kharkov had been a primo piece of real estate. "Your grandparents had a splendid apartment, right in the heart of the city," Babushka always told me. Even Mama herself, who could scarcely bear to hold the word *Kharkov* in her mouth, admitted as much. Of course I couldn't see inside the place, but architecture doesn't lie: the windows were small, the ceilings low, and the balcony held in place with what appeared to be a giant dollop of sticky-tack. It was a squat and ordinary Brezhnev-era flat.

We stood awkwardly in the dirt—the grass having long ago been trampled away—and Cousin Lyonya began counting the windows up from the bottom. He pointed vaguely in the direction of the building's upper right-hand corner.

"See that window? That is where you lived." And then, to fill in the silence a bit, he coughed and added, "I used to visit your father here." Pause. "On many different occasions."

I looked up at a sea of darkened windows and pretended I could see wherever he was pointing.

"Oh right, up there. So that was the apartment, huh?" It was easy now to imagine Mama stuck in this place, hating her in-laws and being hated back, waiting for Papa to come home from guarding the zoo, staring out the window at the stinky Lopan winding its way to someplace even stinkier, and plotting our escape. I made a show of looking around, taking pictures of the only things in sight—a dumpster; a sad, pokey jungle gym; and Cousin Lyonya standing on his patch of dirt, looking for all the world like he wished he were someplace else.

On our way back to the hotel, we decided to cut through Sad Shevchenko, passing the statue of the Ukrainian poet that Papa had so movingly described as "kind of OK" along the way. It was a Sunday afternoon and the park was full of families pushing strollers; packs of young guys sporting crew cuts, acid-washed jeans, and collared t-shirts; and dazzling young women. The women mostly walked in pairs, linked at the elbows or holding hands, their dresses glittering fiercely in the sun. I looked down at myself, feeling like I'd somehow surreptitiously slipped past the park's face-control unit. Cousin Lyonya noticed me staring and snorted.

"Eckh, these people. They come to the park looking for attention. They have absolutely nowhere else to go and nothing to do with themselves."

And I thought: Had my family never left, this would have been my Sunday afternoon. I would have woken up, slipped on something scratchy and sequin-covered, then styled my hair for two leisurely hours before hitting the park. There, my friends and I would patrol the trees like a squadron of mismatched bridesmaids, eyeing the bullet-headed men in ball-hugging jeans, hoping that one of them might impregnate us by age twenty-two . . .

We stopped at a bench not far from Freedom Square where we were supposed to meet Volodya, Papa's best friend from college, and his wife, Inna. Lyonya pulled a packet of photographs and some papers wrapped in a plastic bag from his man purse.

"These are for your father. Some old family artifacts I think he'll find interesting."

I thanked Lyonya and handed him an envelope with the money Papa had asked me to pass along. In the midst of this exchange, Volodya and Inna appeared. A round of handshakes, and a struggle to arrive at a common topic of conversation, ensued. Time, we decided, for some awkward photos together. Then Lyonya told us to come back to Kharkhov again soon, promising to cook us dinner next time. A quick hug and a kiss and he was gone—the Cousin Who No Longer Drinks Water.

Volodya had apparently also gotten a copy of Papa's dismal list of things to do, because as soon as the niceties were over, he turned to me and said, "Okay then, off to the zoo?"

We set off across the square, passing beneath the lengthening shadow of Lenin before cutting through the grounds of the university where Volodya and Inna had studied together with Papa.

"I remember once," Volodya began, "your father and I lucked into finding some money just lying on the sidewalk. A small fortune, something like twenty dollars. So we decided to realize a long-held dream of ours . . ."

Volodya laughed, a bit overcome by the memory, and I imagined a debauched binge of black-market purchases, Papa sitting, pasha-like, atop an illicit blue-jean-and-caviar mountain.

"We set for ourselves," Volodya continued, "the goal of visiting every shashlik stand in Kharkov!"

To me this sounded suspiciously like a quest to visit every Dunkin' Donuts in Worcester, but I did my best to radiate enthusiasm.

"Ambitious!" I chirped.

Volodya was still deep into enumerating the shashlik stands of Kharkov when we reached the iron gates of the Kharkov State Zoo. The zoo's paths were lined with colorful, campy signs that could have been lifted straight from the set of a John Waters movie, but did nothing to hide the state of the animals themselves, who had gone from sad to miserable in Papa's absence. I took off down the darkening, overgrown lane alone, past some dull-eyed bears and a collapsed ostrich, stopping to take a picture of a baboon who looked up at me like he hoped I had some Lexapro.

"I used to talk to them," Papa had told me. "Not the lions, though. They never seemed interested. Also, all of the expensive animals were locked up in a different part of the zoo, so I didn't talk to them either."

I was sorry Papa had to talk to cheap animals.

"That's what you did? All night?"

"No. Just until the other guards came around to see if I had a ruble."

"Did you give it to them?"

"I'd better. One of them was just a drunk, but the other was a man with a past—a former chauffeur in the KGB. He used to drive agents to make their arrests. Sometimes big shots. These kinds of visits . . . well, a lot of people were never heard from again. Anyway, they'd come by on their rounds and we'd pool our money, go drinking."

"What would you say to them?" I'd asked. "I mean the animals."

"I don't know. I just . . . commiserated."

By the time Papa began working at the zoo, he'd been on the blacklist for years. The Ministry of Higher Education had long ago eliminated the graduate position he'd received in physics, a signal that he'd never be allowed to pursue his PhD. He had also quit the Komsomol, a dangerous move for anyone save those who had already given up all hope of a career in the Soviet Union. As the last light faded, I imagined my father there, a young man in a uniform with a gun, staring through the bars, seeking out dark, wet eyes for a few quiet moments of communion. Before the KGB chauffeur came to take him away.

We went back to Volodya's place for dinner—a three-bedroom apartment extravagant by Soviet standards, but which could now merely be considered cozy—to drink vodka and enjoy a lavish feast of mayonnaise-based salads. By the time Volodya and Inna led us back to the hotel it was well past midnight and the windows of the concrete boxes surrounding Freedom Square were lit up like giant grids in an epic game of Battleship.

"I have a present for your father that I've been waiting to give to you," Volodya said. Then he reached into his bag and handed me a book. *One Hundred Famous Kharkovchiani*, it read. Now here was something approximately zero people in my family would have any interest in reading.

"Thanks," I said, but Volodya stopped me before I could put it away.

"First turn to page eighty-four."

I opened the book, and Josh came to look over my shoulder. There, to my amazement, was a grainy black-and-white photograph of Papa and an entry that began:

VILENKIN ALEKSANDR VLADIMIROVICH
(Born 1900–Died 1900)

I looked up at Volodya, whose smile only grew wider as he noted my wonder and confusion.

"The text, of course, is not without some errors."

In late September, I received another note from Kiril: "Hello, Alina it is a journalist of Kiril from Kharkov. Thank you very much for an interview. I wrote about Your desire to come forward in Ukraine and, hope, my words will notice. Here that turned out from our correspondence. In my person in Ukraine another admirer appeared for you." At the bottom of the message, there was a link leading to the *Komsomolskaya Pravda* website. When I clicked on it I found an old photograph of myself in our backyard in North Carolina hovering above Kiril's byline. The article began: *Our countrywoman, daughter of the fa-*

mous physicist Alexander Vilenkin, tells "Komsomol" about how she became a rock star in the United States.

It was an absurd exaggeration. I had released two albums on obscure indie labels and would have been surprised to learn that sales of either had reached into the high three digits. But it only got worse. Whereas Kiril hadn't known who my father was when he'd first contacted me, it was clear he'd done some research since then. Now the article was mostly about Papa. And he sounded like a dissident freedom fighter.

I read on, with growing horror, as weird conjectures flew around like zoons. *Despite the famous father*, the article continued, *Alina has always opened all the doors of life herself. She has never positioned herself as the daughter of the famous scientist, and even appears on stage under the pseudonym Simone.* What was stranger, I wondered, the idea that I would create a pseudonym to outrun undeserved glory should anyone discover my association with the creator of the Theory of Eternal Inflation, or the fact that Kiril, during the course of his extensive research, hadn't managed to discern that Simone was my real last name? But the final straw came when I learned that adopting my alleged pseudonym was also part of a clever ploy to exploit the popularity of Paul *Simon.*

Kiril, I thought to myself. I hate you. I stopped reading and called Papa.

"This is totally embarrassing!" I said. "What if anyone I actually know ever sees this?"

"Well . . ." Papa sighed. "That's what they're supposed to do, isn't it? Make things interesting."

"I would never go around calling myself a rock star."

"And I am a dissident freedom fighter? It doesn't mean anything."

I hung up the phone. Papa was right, it didn't mean anything. Maybe in some parallel universe the Kharkov-shaped hole in my heart could be filled, puzzlelike, by Kharkov itself. Here on planet Earth, I would have to settle for filling it with heat and proper water pressure.

Still, I figured Mama would want to know how the story ended, to see the final result of my "collaboration" with Kiril, so I forwarded the link along. A few hours later, I had my response. I thought she was writing to tell me how pleased she'd been to discover the article included her account of my early childhood, unedited and in its entirety. But all I got was this:

Alina,
Just to let you know, I want an electric tea kettle for Christmas. Mine is leaking.
m.

GLOOM-DEFLECTING
MAILMAN WARRIOR GODS

There were no misspellings. No horrible questions. *Are you the "complete" package? Do you have unique, cutting-edge talent and the follow-through it takes to succeed?* No inscrutable requirements. *Must have full head of hair OR no hair AT ALL.* No pent-up rage. *Fuck whiners, egomaniacs, and slackers. If you aren't 150% serious about making this band a full-time gig then go sit on your fucking finger and ROTATE!!!* No scamming. *Raw, slick, fast, slow, lo-fi, no-fi, hipster, retro, old-school, post-punk, neo-soul . . . I will fill in your blank, rawk star :-))))*

After months of looking for bandmates on Craigslist, it was a relief to find the Producer, a professional who also happened to meet my minimal standard of being sane, polite, and competent. His ad was vague, mentioning only that he was looking for a female singer to collaborate on a new album, but I noticed that he hadn't used the word *collab*, nor did he make any wild, flag-raising claims. Still, I had to admit, the thing that appealed to me most here was that a producer, as opposed to a mere bandmate, had *power*. Something I lacked; something no one else I knew had any of either. True, I had never worked with one, or even met one, but I imagined a producer to be something like the Thomas Cooke of the rock world, riding the rough seas of Craigslist to unearth raw talent, returning to lay treasure at the feet of Tommy Mottola and David Geffen. At the very least, his SoHo address inspired confidence.

It felt like cheating, but I craved a shortcut. Casual encounters of the musical kind had come to dominate my nights and weekends, trapping me in a surreal game of speed dating with a cast of similarly damaged and desperate people. Why were the people I met through Craigslist in New York so different from the easygoing musicians I'd played with when I lived in Austin, the ones I'd found by going to record stores and putting up flyers, just like a medieval person? The people answering my ads now were always the lifers, the ones who used Craigslist as a verb.

"I've been Craigslisting for over a year now," one potential bassist exhaled down into his coffee. "How about you?" And I realized that our meet-up had suddenly transformed into an AA meeting minus the hard chairs. Then there was the rockabilly guitar player who dressed like Elvis and left a trail of cologne in his wake strong enough to disinfect my bathroom. And the girl whose musical taste never pre-dated whatever band had played the Bowery Ballroom the previous night. There was the pale, slumpy guy who hated his tech job working for a financial services firm and doomed every sentence with the preface "As soon as I get my shit together . . ." Not to mention the series of dismal encounters that led to the discovery that New Jersey is home to a cult of male lawyers obsessed with Jeff Buckley. I was ready for all this to end, so when I heard back from the Producer, I felt more than the usual cheap pick-me-up of knowing my credentials had checked out. We agreed to meet up at his space the following Tuesday, and I spent the rest of the week deleting people from my inbox and feeling happy about it.

The studio was in one of those expensive and painfully maintained Manhattan buildings that always look wholly deserted. It was raining the morning of my audition and I'd made the unfortunate decision to eat a croissant along the way, only to notice once I reached the door that it had flaked down the front of my black jacket. I pawed at myself uselessly for a moment, realized it was hopeless, then rang the buzzer for the second floor. Within a moment, the speaker crackled and a clipped male voice came at me.

"Is this my eleven o'clock?"

"Yes."

"Are you the Ricky Lee Jones one or the Annie Lennox one?"

"I . . . sorry?"

"Second flo—" Then the door sang its flat note and there was nothing left to do but open it.

As I stood inside the doorway, wondering what to make of this exchange, a familiar sensation began to creep over me. Let's call it *hope slippage*—the quick drop of pressure when oversized expectations are ratcheted down, violently and without warning. This is going to be bad, a voice inside my head whispered. Run away, while you still can! But I didn't run. I went upstairs, feeling grateful that at least the hallway wasn't mirrored.

The Producer was sitting in an Aeron chair, backlit by an enormous Mac screen. When he got up to greet me I noticed that he was strikingly good-looking: John Edwardsy haircut, belted black pants, and a long-sleeved shirt whose color could best be described as expensive. Everything in the studio looked very modern and new. A 24-channel mixing board without a spot of dust among its matrix of knobs, a sleek desk made of dark wood, a side table with a neat stack of *Tape Op* back issues.

"Helena?" he said, looking down at the list in his hand.

"Alina."

"Well, *Alina*, it must really be throwing it down out there!" he said with a nod at my dripping guitar case. "I forget, did you ever email me that list of influences?"

"I think I mentioned Sinéad O'Connor—"

"*Roight!*" he said, making some notes on his list. "So then *you* must be the Sinéad O'Connor one?"

"Um—" I said, finding it surprisingly difficult to push the words "I am the Sinéad O'Connor one" out of my mouth.

"Why don't you go ahead and set up over there while I finish some things." The Producer pointed to the back wall, where a Marshall stack waited on a square of lintless carpet.

"No problem," I said, and felt it again, that small drowning sensation. I knelt down to thread a daisy chain into my pedals and took the opportunity to give myself a little talk. So what, I said to myself, if this guy doesn't have a very personalized approach to things? I was living in New York City now and would have to accept the fact that not everyone was going to recognize my unique qualities until I actually proved myself. Just keep putting one foot in front of the other. Remember what the inscription said? I had found it a few weeks ago while running errands in the Fashion District: "Neither snow, nor rain, nor heat, nor gloom of night stays these couriers from the swift completion of their appointed rounds." These were words carved into the stone face of the landmark Farley post office, high above the doors. Channel their strength, I thought, the strength of gloom-deflecting mailman warrior gods, pounding the streets of New Amsterdam, carrying out their noble mission without complaint!

"Are we all set here?" The Producer swiveled around to face me, Moleskine open on his lap. He managed to look both bored and expectant at the same time.

"Totally!" I found myself saying, in a false, bright voice that came from nowhere.

And then it all went as shitty as I thought it would.

·

I don't know if it was the cut of the blinds or the recessed lighting or the pristine desk, but as I strummed through the intro I wondered whether the studio had been purposely designed to repel any kind of emotion. It held all the passion and warmth of the toner aisle at Staples. And when I began to sing, I noticed that my voice sounded weirdly thin, as though this were a concert being broadcast, live, from inside a Dixie cup. The Producer watched me while doing tight, controlled half-turns in his Aeron chair. He looked very much as though he was trying hard not to grow a third eye in the back of his head so that he could check his email. Time seemed to move in jagged, stop-gap animation. One second I was fully present, the next my brain had run off in search of someplace less sinister. Now the Producer was writing something down on his notepad. Was that good or bad? I hit the chorus and the heavy bass notes balked at the edge of the carpet, dying an ungraceful death between us. The Producer tapped his pen against his desk. Was he trying to tell me something? Was my timing off? The reasons for going through all of this suddenly seemed very far away. I was in a horror movie and this was a fake office, painted mauve and filled with product placements. The slick, handsome producer was actually an alien tapeworm in nice pants. When he reached over slowly to open a desk drawer, his face would slough off, and then cockroaches would start falling out of the light fixtures. I would think maybe they were just raisins at first until I felt them moving over my bare arms—

Then it was over. The hum of the hard drive and the rattle of the air-conditioner vent were the only sounds. And there was I, a patient lying on the metal table in my paper dress, awaiting diagnosis.

The Producer cleared his throat and clicked the base of a ball-point pen against his desk. He took a last, wistful glance at the computer screen and then turned back around to face me.

"How many albums," he began, "do you suppose PJ Harvey sold in the U.S. last year?" Click, unclick, click.

I stood there for a moment, blinking and wondering what this was all about.

"Lots?" I offered lamely.

The Producer shook his head, a bit sadly.

"Not lots. Not lots at all. Maybe a load for New York or L.A., but forget about the rest of the country." He paused to consider his cell phone, which had started blinking. "You like PJ Harvey, I gather?"

"I do, but—"

"*Roight,*" he interjected. "Well, I'm afraid that's not what this project is all about."

"Can I ask," I said softly, "what exactly *is* this project about?"

He smiled and leaned back in his chair.

"This," he said, sweeping an arm over the mixing board, the city, the world, "is about a second house in the Hamptons. For me."

Then the Producer opened a desk drawer, pulled out a CD, and offered it to me. On the cover was a picture of a girl in a flowy dress, slightly blurred, running across a field. It looked like a still from a tampon commercial. The Producer waited impatiently for me to say something, as though he'd just handed me the clue that would clear up our little misunderstanding.

"Something you produced?" I managed.

"Back in England. I found this Scottish girl and we cut the album in a week. Know how much I cleared on that one?"

I shook my head mutely.

"Fifty. Bloody. Grand. Licensed some of those songs for commercials and never even had to leave the studio."

At this the Producer leaned back in his chair and laughed softly. Not sure what exactly to do with myself, I decided to laugh along with him, like we were in this together, just two people answering the clarion call of second-home ownership.

"Fifty grand is nice, but the only thing it buys you in this town is a parking spot, *roight*?"

I nodded. It was true that you couldn't build a house on a parking spot.

"So this next project has to be bigger, something worth millions. I see blokes with half the smarts pulling it off all the time."

Then there was a soft knock at the door and an older woman with straight blond hair and a posh overcoat stepped into the room.

"Jill!" said the Producer. "Is it that time already? Jill, this is Helena." He waved a hand in my direction and continued, "Jill and I are working on some jingles and were about to step out for tea. Shall we see you downstairs?" It wasn't a question.

As soon as we were outside the building, the Producer held out his hand in parting. "Well, thanks for stopping by," he said. "Cheers!"

"Cheers," I echoed, cheerlessly, turning back toward the subway. With a sinking heart, I considered the picture of myself in an hour, face bathed in laptop glow, scanning Craigslist for posts ending "only serious inquiries please." If my father, the scientist, were here, I thought as I walked, he would remind me that success is only a matter of statistics and that pessimism is an illogical response to failure. Failure only means that you haven't thrown yourself, face-first, against the brick wall of probability enough times. And to quit after only one try? That would be committing statistical suicide.

Take the story of Papa's good friend Zhenya Chudnovsky. Chudnovsky was a fellow physicist from Kharkov, a refusenik who had spent more than eleven years trying to convince the Soviet government to let him leave. In 1987, Papa wrote a letter to Gorbachev, asking that Chudnovsky be allowed to emigrate, and started gathering the signatures of prominent American physicists. After he had collected more than a hundred signatures, Papa called Senator Ted Kennedy to see whether he might present the letter to Gorbachev on his upcoming visit to the Soviet Union. Kennedy's staff agreed to have the letter delivered, so Papa went ahead and mailed it to the senator's office in Boston. After Kennedy returned from his trip, Papa called to find out whether he had in fact given the letter to Gorbachev but couldn't get any response from Kennedy's office. He began to leave increasingly shrill messages until finally, months later, someone on Kennedy's staff admitted that the senator had never presented the letter to Gorbachev, because the letter had been lost—the original copy with all of the signatures. So Papa started over again with a photocopy of the letter, this time turning north to New Hampshire for help. Governor John Sununu agreed to present the letter to Gorbachev, and it worked; Chudnovsky and his family were released. When my parents went to visit him a few days after his arrival in the United States, they found Chudnovsky standing in the middle of an apartment that was totally empty save for a New Hampshire flag the size of a parachute tacked to the wall. A gift from John Sununu.

What if Papa hadn't tried again with Sununu? Or what if he had stopped at just ten signatures? Even fifty? Then maybe Chudnovsky would have remained stuck in Kharkov, left to take Papa's place manning the kiosk at Café Lira just off Shevchenko Park. I could suddenly picture him there, his uniform worn to a dull shine, drinking industrial alcohol from a plastic cup and spitting *semechki* on the frozen ground with barely repressed brutality.

But maybe Papa's laws of probability did not apply to me— maybe they applied only to people like Papa, who had noble goals and the iron-plated constitution necessary to pursue them. My goals were small and ignoble: to record some songs, to play a Tuesday-night show at Arlene Grocery, to be a person whose ambitions weren't best described using air quotes. Was it even worth a struggle? I could always go back to living with the low-grade shame of having a dream in life and doing nothing to pursue it. It was a common-enough affliction to live with, like dandruff or a deviated septum. Certainly a far distant cousin to that other kind of shame, the kind that confronts you directly in the form of rejections that are blunt, damaging, and Google-searchable. Coming to New York to become a singer had only made me realize exactly how fine a palate for humiliation one could develop, and how quickly. It was as though I had unknowingly signed up for some kind of twisted Iron Chef competition in which shame turns out to be the surprise ingredient. There were countless subtle variations on a few persistent themes: the shame of not being good enough, of secretly wanting something from someone, of pretending to like people you don't like, of rejection, of self-doubt, of looking like a poseur, of being too ambitious or not ambitious enough . . .

Papa clearly had the inner strength to endure defeat and triumph—but me? I had all the resilience of a slug being introduced to a nice teaspoon of sea salt. The fatal flaw, I thought, must lie in my upbringing, in the fact that Papa had grown up forging his character against the whetting stone of a totalitarian regime, whereas I had grown up in the Reagan-era suburbs of Massachusetts, wondering why the sprinklers were always left running in the rain.

In my family you learned to solve your own problems. Perhaps this was because the Soviet Union just wasn't a place that coddled its weak or troubled—personal issues requiring anything short of a visit to an asylum were typically self-medicated away with vodka, dubious herbal remedies, or emigration. Besides, the kinds of problems I had growing up in America were not even things my family remotely recognized as problems. It was as though I were pointing out mushrooms from the window of an airplane. I would complain about my lack of ponies, my seemingly genetic inability to learn French, their unreasonable refusal to send me to five-thousand-dollar summer camps for the performing arts, and they would consider my words with a preoccupied and distant air.

"Yes, life is hard, isn't it?" my father would say, without looking up from his lined pad of yellow paper. My father, who had been denied any kind of livelihood in our native Kharkov, who'd been blacklisted by the KGB and sent to serve hard labor with convicts, who had arrived in the United States knowing no one, with a young family and one hundred dollars to his name, who then completed his PhD in physics in just one year, would shake his head. "Sorry to hear about gym class. But you're very resourceful. I'm sure you'll find a way to manage."

Sometimes I would take my complaints to Babushka, who lived in nearby Cambridge. Babushka's father had died fighting for the White Army when she was an infant, and she spent her first seven years in hiding with her mother in the small town of Sevsk, where they lived in constant fear that the authorities would discover their "bourgeois" background. Her first husband died at the front, during World War II, leaving her to endure the Siege of Leningrad, watching aunts and cousins die slowly of starvation, before finally escaping to Kyrgyzstan. I would come over to recount my various grievances and Babushka would sit at the dining room table, watching me with ancient eyes, listening quietly. When I was done, she might pause for a moment and then push a bowl of cold strawberries across the table.

"Lastochka," she would say, with an encouraging smile. "These aren't quite ripe yet so try them with some sugar."

Perhaps it was precisely because I had nothing to oppose or protest, no wars or famines to suffer through, no evil idealogues to oppress me, that I was anxious. It started with the houses, specifically the mansions. The big, imposing Colonials and Victorians and the brick compounds of a more recent vintage that could easily be confused for the embassy of some Mediterranean country. I walked past a stretch of them every day on the way to school, my worries only growing as the grand parade of stately manors, laced with snow like exquisite pastries, unspooled before me one by one. It seemed that somehow by going to school, and then going to college, and then getting a job, I was expected to come back to a place like this and acquire an impossibly terrific and expensive house. True, nobody had ever poked me in the chest and made this particular declaration, but the implication was always there, built into the suggestion that perhaps I reconsider dropping that AP history class. All I had to do was look around and learn by example. My parents had pulled themselves up out of nothing, acquiring a sizable mortgage and a Honda several cuts above a Civic. They had filled entire photo albums with pictures of themselves riding llamas in places I could not pronounce. Their Russian friends were similarly accomplished, having all invented a magical, cash-producing piece of math that lived inside a computer. It came as no surprise, then, that their children were the straight-A students, the violin prodigies and science fair winners, the shitty athletes and social misfits with untamable hair and oversized lips, waiting with barely concealed bwahahas for the day when they would rule the world.

Only I knew exactly how doomed I was. There were faint assurances from different quarters that it was only a matter of time, my innate ability to solve integral equations and calculate the torque of falling objects on the moon was bound to surface sooner or later. Out of all my relatives who had emigrated to the States from the Soviet Union, the only person without a PhD in the sciences was my loser mother, who'd only managed to drag her slacker ass through a masters in physics. But as I sat there, listlessly sniffing rocks in earth science class and trying to determine their salinity, I knew it just wasn't true. I would never wake up one day alive with the feeling that the Bunsen burner was a life-altering piece of equipment that must somehow be integrated into my daily routine. No, the only thing that I really cared about was singing and writing songs. I wanted to write songs just like Sinéad O'Connor's. Not the ones that made her famous—the other ones. But since this rather specific subject matter wasn't covered at school, I had the gnawing feeling that I would get stuck doing something else when I grew up, something grim and joyless and papery. And I worried that I would end up as bitter and bitten as the school secretaries with the lipstick-stained teeth, standing outside by the fire door and glaring at us as they sucked the last dregs of youthful desire up through a Lucky Strike.

Looking back, I see only missed opportunities for just merrily going off the rails. Once a person has been declared a human castastrophe, any move they make is pretty much considered a move up. Perhaps against the grim backdrop of a life spent living in hotels that charge by the hour, my goal of becoming a rock singer would have been reframed as a fine and healthful step forward. Besides, if things didn't work out, youth was always the best possible insurance policy for eventual forgiveness.

I had it all laid out in my head; the only problem was I lacked guts. My plan was simple. First, I would camouflage myself using the oceanic quantities of eye makeup that lived in the medicine cabinet behind Mama's bathroom mirror. Then I would walk the mile from my house to historic Mass. Ave. and take the 56 bus to Alewife just like Paul Revere. From there it was but a short subway ride on the Red Line to Harvard Square, where some casual inquiries among the kids hanging out in the Pit would earn me a place on the floor of an Allston squat with eighteen roommates and a bunch of cats that no one took care of. I would get a job waitressing at Wursthaus, the bar where I'd once successfully ordered a vodka and cranberry juice at age fourteen, and save enough money to buy an electric guitar. At this point, the route to stardom would naturally reveal itself. My parents would be devastated by my disappearance, of course, but they could always adopt a girl from Russia who would surely make a much better ballerina.

I didn't run away, though. I kept my head down, went to college with a lukewarm feeling in my heart, and generally did all the things that were required of me. To do otherwise would have meant enduring Mama's hemorrhoidal screaming, Papa's quiet disappointment, and Babushka's potential heart attacks. I fulfilled my duties well enough to stay afloat, but never well enough to distinguish myself. Yet long after I'd moved away from Lexington, I still felt the weight of its houses. I graduated from college, moved to Austin, but always returned home to pointed conversations about my low-paying jobs and lack of direction. Arriving at the door, Mama would always greet me wearing the same necklace, a familiar family heirloom. This was the last remnant of my great-great-grandmother's waist-length lorgnette chain, a piece of finely woven gold that had been passed through generations, then cut down and traded for food during the Siege of Leningrad until just this small piece remained. At some point after the dinnertime conversation had dwindled to the polite clink of teacups and saucers, Mama would inevitably take the chain in one hand and absentmindedly start twisting it around one finger.

"You know," she would say to me, with a meaningful look, "one day this necklace is going to be yours."

And I felt the weight of that too.

•

After my encounter with the Producer I took a long break from Craigslist, preferring to spend my time writing songs in the bedroom of my Hoboken apartment and performing them for an exclusive audience of cats. Eventually, though, I did get my shit together. I paired up with a cellist recruited through a flyer tacked up at Maxwell's and a drummer I found on Craigslist to form a scruffy little band called Disfarmer. We recorded some demos, played a few shows around the city, and were denounced as "Bjdorklike" by Chuck Eddy in *The Village Voice*. It was finally looking as though all my modest dreams were coming true, until one day my cellist announced she was moving to D.C. and a few months later the band fell apart. I found myself right back where I'd started, at the beginning of another miserable hunt for bandmates on Craigslist. I realized it could easily take the better part of a year just to reach my previous high-water mark of being called Bjdorklike. This thought was dreary enough to consider, but now there was the other problem as well. The problem of the ultimatum.

It happened while I was living in Austin, moving through a series of office jobs that carried me effortlessly toward a very specific career that I didn't want. I woke up one day to a deepening state of misery and the sudden vision of my future as a big, rambling house out of a Brontë novel set on fire, the prospects for escape narrowing as each hallway filled with smoke. My panic crescendoed until one night I finally called Papa, my words all tumbling out in a bitter rush, like I'd just drunk a cup of acid and had only four seconds to live. I explained that I'd made all the wrong choices in life because I was too scared—scared of performing, scared of asking for help, scared of failing at the only thing I really want to do with my life. Wasn't it sad, Papa, that I'd missed the chance to do so many things? That I would never be an Olympic gymnast or president of the United States or Yo-Yo Ma? Papa listened quietly to my rant, and when I was done, he firmly agreed with me that I should at least try singing, otherwise I would always regret it. But being a practical person, he also gave me the following ultimatum: You have until you are twenty-five to do something with your music. After that, he all but said, it would be time to get about the business of living up to other people's expectations.

When I hung up the phone the world seemed different. It was true that as a student, the imposition of an arbitrary and cruel deadline always had the tonic effect of rejuvenating my determination. But this time it had the opposite effect and I froze, becoming a veritable human Popsicle of indecision. When I brought up the ultimatum with Papa many years later, he said, "I didn't *give* you that ultimatum—I just strongly suggested *you* give *yourself* that ultimatum."

"Wow." I was full of doubts on that score. "You'll have to forgive me for totally misinterpreting you like that."

"Either way," he added, chortling, "I don't regret it."

But after Disfarmer broke up, no one was chortling at the ultimatum. I was already two years behind schedule—a twenty-seven-year-old disappointment. How would I ever catch up? Jonesing again for the quick fix, I did what I swore I would never do again and answered an ad posted on Craigslist by another producer: George from Brooklyn. A week later I found myself on a Coney Island–bound F train, rattling toward one of those ill-defined neighborhoods where the streets all trail off into endless chorus lines of fix-a-flats and scratch ticket bodegas.

I guessed that maybe the neighborhood where I was headed was one of those obscure corners of Brooklyn where young artists, rent-hike refugees from Williamsburg and Greenpoint, find cheap apartments with high ceilings. All those shuttered, sunken storefronts below probably opened to reveal soaring lofts with shag carpeting stapled to the walls, I thought to myself. And for some reason I'd already formed a mental image of the hipster who would greet me at the station. He'd be wearing a vintage World Party t-shirt, thrift store jeans, and an old pair of Vans. He'd have the five o'clock goatee and the bleary look of someone who'd spent most of his day scouring eBay for deals on discontinued toy Casio keyboards. But I couldn't have been further off the mark. The man who met me at the station was much older than I was, with a pockmarked face and watery eyes. He wore a faded army jacket and a logoless baseball cap pulled down almost to his eyes. George, I realized, was the kind of guy who immediately makes you feel sketchy just by association.

From his hello, it seemed like I had already done something vaguely annoying just by showing up at the station. He took my guitar with an exasperated yank that said, Come on, you know you'll end up hurting your ovaries if I let you carry that. Then he told me that his real name was Georgi and he had come to the States from Tbilisi with help from Jewish Family Services. I waited for an opening to tell him that I was born in Kharkov and we both spoke Russian, but he never stopped talking. It was the familiar patois of failure: a first wife, then a second, an estranged daughter now grown and studying business administration at Baruch, a revoked cabbie license, too many moves from the blurry edges of one borough to another. He sucked hard on an unfiltered cigarette and walked hunched into it like he was afraid I might snatch it from his mouth and run away laughing.

Georgi's studio smelled like burnt brownies. It had dismally low ceilings and was crammed with books, vinyl, heaps of clothes, tea bags hardened into the bottoms of stray cups, and pillows fat with cigarette smoke. It was as though a spaceship from Planet Lonely Bachelor had crashed right here, into a dumpy fourth-floor walk-up in south Brooklyn. He walked over to a bed submerged in old synthesizers and tangled cables piled so high that they blocked much of the light from the room's only window, and cleared a space. Then he sat down on the bed and motioned me over. I didn't really want to sit next to him on the sour-smelling sheets—it made me feel like I'd answered a different kind of ad—but there didn't seem to be any alternative.

"Sit!" Georgi barked. So I sat. Then Georgi grabbed a framed photo from the nightstand and pushed it into my hands.

"First of all, this is Stacey." Unlike everything else, the frame wasn't dusty. I could tell the shot had been taken at the downstairs bar of Acme Underground, one of the city's crappier starter clubs. There was a perky blond girl smiling and then half of Georgi's head sailing out of the frame, leaving only one deranged blue eye.

"Who is Stacey?"

"She was my partner, until last year."

"She moved?" I asked.

"We fell out. And then she left for California. On a bike. Here's another one, with the fucking bike."

He plucked another dustless photo from the inner frame of a mirror. I barely glanced at it—a girl on a motorcycle—before handing it back.

"Now pick a track number so I can play you something of ours. One? Nine? Seven?"

"Uh, seven?"

"I will play you track six. Six is better."

Georgi punched at the stereo and the music started: a sugary keyboard run, the chug of programmed drums, a familiar bass line. Then came the girl's voice, totally uncomplicated. It wasn't *bad* exactly, it was just the kind of music that automatically shut my brain off. If this song were a feeling, I thought, it would be the feeling of standing in line at Starbucks, waiting for a half-caff latte while checking out the overpriced mugs. And the words were awful.

When it ended, Georgi reached for a cigarette.

"Not bad," I said wanly.

"Can I just tell you something?" Georgi lit the cigarette, not bothering with the window, and went on, "I know that Americans don't like honesty, but please, allow me to talk, okay? You will have to know how it is if we are going to work together. Understand this: if Stacey walked back in here today, even after everything that happened, I would take her back without any questions. Sorry, I wouldn't care whose ass was in here. *Vot tak.*" He reached down for a dirty coffee mug to ash into and continued, "Now I *will* tell you that the next girl won't be such a fucking mess, with the jealous boyfriends and the brother always turning up at the apartment with some kind of 'emergency.'"

Was it my imagination or did someone just cue the creepy background music? Had Stacey and Georgi been lovers, I wondered? Was he some kind of stalker? Somehow I didn't get the sense that Georgi was actually dangerous, though my only evidence for this theory was that the books, records, and bad paintings on the wall somehow didn't fit my Martha Stewart blueprint for psychopath home decor.

Georgi jumped up and began pacing up and down on the rug. "I have my theories about what was going on too. She wouldn't answer calls for days, sometimes a week, and then come up with some bullshit story: 'I went to City Island for the weekend.' 'Is that right?' I would say. Do you consider me some kind of idiot? I mean this is New York City—who turns their cell phone off for the weekend? Am I that stupid? What do you think? Do I look like a total idiot to you?"

What I thought was that Russians really loved that word: *idiot*. It was like an honorary pronoun. Then I did whatever one does in these situations: shook my head, did my best impression of a sympathetic look. I wondered how far things could actually go before I overcame the constraints of politeness, picked myself up, and walked out the door. As if in response to this internal question, Georgi sat back down heavily, knees thrust out, and checked his watch.

"Shit, it's already three thirty," he said, taking out another cigarette and tapping it on the inside of his wrist. "Play me something."

I stood there uncertainly, staring down into the furry crack between the wall and the bed.

"What? Do you need a water or something?"

It occurred to me that the fastest way to get out of there was just to do as Georgi asked. Even though he'd never explained what it was, exactly, that I was auditioning for, I had a feeling it was best not to know and stood up to get my guitar. While I set up, Georgi sat there in his stained pants atop a tangle of wires on the bed, waving the smoke away from his face. Though poignant and memorable in its own way, it was the kind of little scene that somehow never gets immortalized in a snow globe. I took a breath and sang a song that I'd written a long time ago, about a girl in a bad situation.

This time I didn't wait around to hear a verdict when I was done; I just bent down to unplug my tuning pedal and began stuffing my guitar back into its case. Georgi watched me pack my things wordlessly. It was suddenly very quiet, except for the radiator making wet, dying noises.

"It seems to me," he said slowly, "that you have your own thing going on."

"I guess," I said.

"So do you need me or not?"

It was an oddly dramatic thing to say and implied a level of intimacy that I hoped we'd never attain. Nonetheless, I decided to make the most of my Katharine Hepburn moment. I took the handle of my guitar case, straightened up, and raised my chin. I looked Georgi in the eyes.

"Um . . . maybe?" I said.

"Then let's go," said Georgi, tossing his cigarette butt into the dirty mug. "I have another girl to meet at the train."

Waiting for the F on the elevated platform, I pulled out my cell phone and called Ben, a friend of mine from back home who had just finished his MFA and moved to Brooklyn to make it as a video artist. We had a habit of calling each other to complain whenever things went badly, which is another way of saying that we were always in touch.

"Ben, I'm such a loser," I said as soon as he picked up the phone. I'd felt ready to yammer on for hours, but found myself running out of things to say after fifteen seconds. Apparently nothing had actually happened.

"Whatever, dude," Ben began—because everyone who grows up in Massachusetts tries to mask their lack of familiarity with the sun by adopting the vocabulary of a surfer—"sounds like that guy's just a douchebag. Another douchebag in a sea of douchebags." Then Ben excused himself to go finish up a video starring a toy pony head on a stick. He'd shown the toy to me the last time I'd come over. When you pulled the pony's ear it whinnied, "I like it when you brush me!" in a creepy electronic voice. I let Ben go. I understood; he was busy and had parents of his own to disappoint. The F train arrived and I settled into a window seat, pressing my cheek against the scratchiti as it pulled away from Kings Highway. *Neither snow, nor rain, nor heat, nor gloom of night stays these couriers from the swift completion of their appointed rounds.* Swinging out over Brooklyn, above miles of brick and concrete and soapstone-faced buildings rolling out to the horizon, I had to admit: the odds were against me.

Maybe my fatal flaw had been that I'd set the bar too high, measuring myself against the expectations of people born with dictator-defying superpowers. The mailmen would make for more appropriate role models. The mailmen weren't facing a hail of bullets or trying to feed a family on one potato a day. Theirs were ordinary problems—crotchety old ladies, July thunderstorms, hungry dogs. A bag of mail and one day to distribute it; this was the kind of challenge even someone like me could cope with, given the proper footwear. As the train passed Ditmas Avenue I noticed that I should have been feeling terrible, but somehow, felt okay. I was a directionless twenty-seven-year-old facing a dwindling probability of success, but hey, at least I didn't share the final bottom-feeding rung of the Craigslist ladder with someone like Georgi. There is a certain peace that comes with the realization you aren't ruining anyone else's life but your own. I pondered this strange new calm and wondered: Had I just limboed below that final humiliation threshold, beyond which nothing else could hurt me? Had my resolve finally hardened, like the feet of some fire-walking swami? Was my luck about to change? There was no answer to these questions or to the question of what to do next. Nothing left to do now but enjoy the view until the train dipped back underground and carried me on toward Manhattan, where even with the weight of the whole city over my head, I wouldn't feel a thing.

DOWN AND OUT ON HOPE STREET

I should have known better. For one thing, they were very, very young, these people with the new record label. They had the blond, healthful look of the kids I never spoke to in high school, and after meeting them for the first time I referred to them forevermore as "the children." I had no idea how they found me. They just appeared one day at the Carrboro Music Festival, to catch a show I was playing in the back of a coffee shop. This show is what convinced them that I should be the first artist they signed. And wasn't that flattering? Wasn't that exciting? I had to admit . . . maybe it was.

I was getting tired. It had been a long, hard year full of near misses. A year is a long time to sit on an album, especially your first. Recording it hadn't been easy. I'd had to go back to New York, where my producer, Steve, let me crash for six weeks in his studio while I rehearsed with my band. The studio was housed in an abandoned storefront, its doors covered in graffiti, its windows cased in iron bars. The building faced a church—the Universal Outreach Ministries of Deliverance—and a sign that read, "Come unto me all ye that labor and are heavy laden and I will give thee rest." Outside men patrolled the street, hawking car stereo parts, often with the wires still trailing from the back. The place was little more than a cavernous squat and it had no heat. When I arrived, in mid-October, it was already cold. By the time I left it was freezing. I often practiced and recorded wearing a coat and scarf, warming my hands on a mug filled with boiled water between takes. There was no one to complain to—Steve had already been living this way for five years.

But at least while I was recording I was driven by a sense of purpose. Once we were done, I had no idea what to do. I had no manager, no label, no booking agent, no anyone. Knowing that it wasn't bound to do much good, I tried contacting labels myself, sending polite, to-whom-it-may-concern notes to "info@" email addresses. At the same time, a few supportive journalists reached out to industry people on my behalf. After a few months of this, with the relatively vague, or in some cases quite explicit, encouragement of a handful of label owners and manager types, I set off on tour, hoping to impress one of them with a live show. But invariably the bigwigs never showed. Or if they did, they slipped off without a word while the lights were still dim. The hot leads grew cold. Rejections poured in. Not knowing what else to do, I got in touch with Lea, a well-respected publicist in New York who liked my work, for advice. She told me that a good music lawyer should be able to help shop my record and gave me a list of lawyers to contact who didn't charge hefty upfront retainers.

Of the five lawyers I contacted, two expressed interest in working with me but not before seeing me perform live. I hastily booked a show at Sin-é on the Lower East Side, and a few weeks later got in the car for the now-familiar drive from Carrboro to New York City. That night, it began to snow. By the following day the storm had exceeded all expectations, dumping more than two feet of snow in Central Park within the span of twenty-four hours and metastasizing into the biggest nor'easter in the city's history. One of the lawyers wrote to tell me he couldn't make it to the show—his flight from Seattle had been canceled. The mood at Sin-é was grim when I arrived that night, the bartender polishing an empty bar, the stage manager busy stage managing nothing but a depopulated void of joy. Aside from a few fearless friends, the club was deserted, and so I sang into the blinding lights, knowing only darkness lay behind them. When I was done, I made my way to the back of the club, where the other lawyer was waiting. He watched me approach, unsmiling.

"Let me ask you something," the lawyer began, without introduction. "What kind of label are you looking to sign to?"

I thought about it for a moment and then named a decent mid-sized indie, one I liked a lot but whose bands most people had probably never heard of.

The lawyer snorted into his drink. "I hate to be the one to tell you this, but you have a long way to go before a label like that would consider signing you."

As the lawyer enumerated all the reasons he couldn't represent me—my songs all sounded the same, I had no stage presence, my lack of hit singles—it dawned on me that he didn't hate being the one to tell me all this. That he was, quite visibly, delighted to be the one to tell me. And as he wound down, I considered the awfulness of getting back to Brooklyn with all my gear and wondered whether I should just cab it straight to the Universal Outreach Ministries of Deliverance. I was certainly heavy laden and badly in need of rest.

Finally noticing I was looking the slightest bit shattered, the lawyer's tone softened.

"Listen, I know how it is. I used to be a musician myself," he said. "I love music. I even named my daughter after a Kinks song."

Reassured that the lawyer loved music—just not mine—I stumbled outside, where I promptly slipped on the ice and dropped my prized tube amp into a snowbank.

So by the time the children "discovered" me, my capacity for trust was much depleted and I'd all but given up on the music industry. Yet I couldn't help but find their enthusiasm infectious. Flock Records, they called themselves. "Come join the Flock!" they cried out happily. But no one knew who the Flock was. The Flock had never flown anywhere before, not even a lazy circle around the perimeter of Greensboro, where they'd apparently hatched. Still, they didn't blink at the cost when I insisted on high-quality packaging, on full radio and print promotion, on tour support. The children had money, and that was good, right? But they didn't have *jobs* and had only just graduated from college, so where did they get that money? I couldn't ask them where the money came from. You can never ask anyone where the money comes from. You want to, but you can't. So I would drive out to Greensboro and meet up with the children at the Green Bean on South Elm Street and we would talk about promo and printers and distribution and every other sweet thing under the sun, except for where the fuck all their money was coming from.

The night before leaving for a three-week tour in Europe, the children came to meet me at the Cat's Cradle in Carrboro, where my band was opening for a faded nineties alt-rocker. I gave them the masters for my album and the original artwork for the cover. We went over all of the contents of the envelope together and then they each gave me a warm hug. By the time I returned to North Carolina, they assured me, the manufactured copies of my album would be ready. They told me that I rocked. I told them they flocked. We said goodbye.

Two weeks later, twenty minutes before I was set to go on stage at a club in Reims, France, I received a message from one of the children that began "I don't quite know how to put this" and went on to explain that all of their capital, $43,000—an amount they kept in cash for "obvious reasons"—had just been stolen by their partner, leaving them without enough money to cover this month's rent, let alone put out my album. I reread the message again and again, wondering if I had missed something. I mean—hello?—was there anything "obvious" about why someone would keep $43,000 in cash hidden in, like, a peanut butter jar under the bed, and not a *bank* like everybody else? I was devastated. I had told everyone I knew that my album was coming out and now all of those people would have to be untold. They would ask me what had happened, and I would have to repeat this story again and again until it became some kind of cautionary fable. "The Indie Rocker and the Hare." Or, "The Boy Who Cried Flock."

Even worse, I was back to square one with the album—the album no one wanted. My thoughts turned black. Wanting something and having nothing: these two ordinary conditions have a terrible binding energy, like matter and antimatter, that under pressure will accelerate and collide. I was a bomb in a briefcase, a terribly violent, ticking thing housed in an ordinary shell that somehow managed to smile, eat food, and carry on conversations as though nothing had happened. On some level, I understood that now was not the time to make hasty decisions; it was the time to stop, think, reassess, chant *Om Shanti*, look at the bigger picture, assert this was just a minor ripple in the whirlpool of life and that no one had died, remember? Yet some irreversible process had been set into motion.

By the time I got back to the States I'd made up my mind: I was leaving North Carolina. True, I was the one guilty of letting hope and naïveté cloud my better judgment. True, the children were incompetent at best, the doe-eyed masterminds of an international crime syndicate at worst. But the real villain here, I'd decided, was North Carolina, where nothing good had ever happened for me and nothing good ever would. My resentment was already long simmering. Josh and I had moved down south only so that he could take a job at the university, and though I'd managed to keep freelancing for my old job back in New York, I found telecommuting isolating and lonely. Without any friends or family within nine hours' driving distance, I spent my first year in Carrboro utterly homesick. Everything felt foreign: the sweet humid air, the breathing carpets of kudzu strewn across the rolling hills, the families of deer that traipsed through our backyard each day, grazing the past owner's abandoned vegetable garden to the ground. One night, not long after we'd arrived, Josh took me out to a nice restaurant in town. It was warm outside, so we had dinner on the back patio, under the stars. When I returned home, I discovered a deer tick stuck to my bare leg. Now, coming from New York City, I was no stranger to vermin. The sight of a mouse or cockroach skirting the wall of a restaurant was hardly enough to merit interrupting a meal. And once, stepping out of some dive in Chinatown, a rat had run over my foot. But as urban encounters with wildlife go, this somehow felt worse. As I pulled the tick's pincers out of my leg, I thought to myself: I miss that rat.

The thing I didn't expect, though, was how much I missed water. Oceans, rivers, lakes. I had lived near water all my life and suddenly felt as though I'd simply been folded into an endless tube of tree wallpaper. Green is a beautiful color until it stabs you relentlessly in the eye all day long, closing in with all the monotony of a cucumber-only diet. I'd heard that there was an artificial lake about a half-hour drive south from our place in Carrboro, but "artificial lake" had a scary, Ray Bradbury–ish ring to it. Stubbornly, I held out for a real lake with actual water.

Then I discovered there *was* a real river nearby, the Neuse, but a quick browse on the internet turned up a very unfortunate piece of news: in 1999, Hurricane Floyd flooded the lagoons of the state's numerous hog farms, dumping 120 million gallons of pig shit into six of North Carolina's major rivers, including the Neuse. This led to the spawning of something called *Pfiesteria piscicida*, a microbe that gnaws giant holes through fish and which *The New York Times* once described as "something out of a horror movie." What did *Pfiesteria piscicida* have to do with the children or my album or anything, really? Nothing. But suddenly, after my record deal fell apart, I decided that I could not stand to live another minute in the microbe's vicinity. I was sick of it all: the trees, the humidity, the Bible school advertisements informing me that God Doesn't Have a Computer but He Can Still Answer Knee-Mail. I was tired of the awesome independent record stores, the club owners who always went out of their way to help me, the supportive local media, and nice Southern people in general. I was a seething ball of hate and all I wanted was to get back to the Northeast, where this quality would be most appreciated. Not forever, just for six weeks.

But what about leaving Josh? Poor Josh. He had been so excited when the children offered to put out my album—perhaps even more excited than I was—and had such great hopes that this would finally give me a feeling of belonging that I had lacked since we moved down to Carrboro. When he read the message from the children, he put his head in his hands and stayed that way for a very long time. He knew it was only a matter of time until my inevitable meltdown. So Josh gave me his blessing—I could leave and we would reunite in New York for the holidays, only three weeks away—but with one caveat.

"Since you're clearly freaking out, I just think it's very important that whatever happens, we remember to be nice to each other."

"I'm not freaking out!" I said shrilly.

"You are," he continued. "So just remember: be nice."

I decided I would rent an apartment in Brooklyn. I didn't know Brooklyn all that well, but I had two good friends, Ben and Eugene, who lived in Park Slope. Sitting at my desk in Carrboro, I found a nice apartment in Park Slope on Craigslist. It was a one bedroom, and in the photos the place looked good—maybe a little girly for my taste, but tidy and well furnished. I exchanged two emails with a woman named Priscilla before sending her a check. Once the deal was done, I forwarded Ben and Eugene a note with my new address. A few hours later, my phone rang.

"Did you even bother to look at a map?" It was Ben.

"What do you mean?" I asked.

"This apartment isn't in Park Slope, it's in Red Hook."

"But the ad *said* Park Slope."

"The ad lied. I'm looking at Google Maps right now."

"It's not in the Slope?" I struggled with this new piece of information. "Well, what's in Red Hook, then? Isn't Red Hook supposed to be, like, the next new place?"

"Maybe, but not where you're living. Hang on . . . I just sent you the link. Check your email. You got it? Now put it in 'satellite' view. And zoom in all the way. Okay, so see all those big blocks over on the left? That's the Red Hook Houses. And then see your place, just across the street over here? It looks the same, right? Dude, I think you just got yourself a place in the projects."

I stared down at all the little rectangles of washed-out rose and gray and green and understood nothing at all. The only thing I understood was that I had to get out of North Carolina. Now. Even if what Ben was saying was true, I was still going. And who said the projects were even a bad place to live?

"Well, I guess I'll have to make it an adventure," I announced cheerfully.

"Did you already pay that lady? Because seriously—"

"Forget it," I interrupted. "I'll see you in a couple weeks. Dude."

I arrived in New York a few days before my sublet began and crashed at Ben's, who had exiled himself to his girlfriend's apartment in Chelsea. With nothing better to do, I decided to drive out to Red Hook for a look at the new place. But as I approached the building, I experienced something I hadn't felt for a long time in New York City: fear. Nearby fences were tipped with barbed wire and the check-cashing joint on the corner sported more armor than a Wells Fargo delivery truck. There was a dark, scary stretch of underpass that whispered, *rape me*. And the building itself did look suspiciously like public housing, which meant my sublet was totally illegal. Unless, of course, Mid-Twentieth-Century Institutional just happened to be this private builder's architectural style of choice. I circled the block two times and then drove back to Ben's apartment, thinking, Well, I'll just have to make sure I'm always home by sundown and have enough food and water to last until morning; it will be good practice for World War III.

The next morning Priscilla called.

"I'm just calling to say that everything's okay," she said, and I knew right away something was wrong. "There's just a . . . a *situation* that's developed with the girl I have here now. She complained about the mail and I got a call from the super. So things are a little, you know, *hot* right now. I was thinking it would be better if you waited a few extra days before moving in."

"Um, maybe. I don't know. That might be okay." It wasn't such an unreasonable request, to wait a few more days.

"I mean, *everything's cool*, it's just so they can see I'm still living here," she added. "But the other thing? After you move in? Is I'm going to have to be hanging around the place for a while . . ."

"What do you mean, 'hanging around'?"

"In case the super comes by. I won't get in your way. Figure I'll just come by to watch some TV, make like I'm cooking something in the kitchen . . . we'll tell him you're my cousin, visiting from North Carolina."

Cousins? I tried to absorb this, but whatever mental sponge I usually kept handy for bizarre pronouncements had long since become saturated. Setting aside that Priscilla was black and I was white, even if we turned out to be twins separated at birth, what about the fact that we had *never met* and *knew nothing about each other*? How was I supposed to prepare for my new role as Priscilla's cousin? Should I head over there now for a marathon session of the Newlywed Board Game, to learn whether she preferred plastic to wooden coat hangers, and what her favorite sex-themed cocktail was?

I told her the deal was off, then sat alone in Ben's apartment, a molelike railroad that came equipped, I swear, with a light/heat/joy destroyer mounted to the living room's only window, waiting for Priscilla to drive over and drop off my check. Somewhere behind the refrigerator, Otto, the feral cat Ben brought home from a Brooklyn alley, radiated anxiety, waiting for me to leave so he could dash out to his bowl for another mouthful of brown food balls. What should I do? I'd already told my boss I'd be in the office on Monday. But I couldn't keep imposing on Ben. Or Otto. Nor could I bear the thought of turning around and driving back to North Carolina. There was really no option but to find another sublet, fast. So I hit Craigslist again, this time narrowing my search to AVAIL NOWs in any borough, and right away made an appointment with someone equally desperate, a girl named Sarah whose roommate had suddenly decided to ditch New York for California. The place was in Williamsburg, almost an hour-long trip from my friends in Park Slope. But the building was on Hope Street, which I could only take as a good omen.

It was nothing more than a giant plaster box, the playground for a landlord who worshipped a fickle god of interior design. There were no shelves in the kitchen, or pantry, just a bookcase filled with cereal boxes propped against a wall. The bathroom was an afterthought, a cube jutting awkwardly into the combined kitchen/living room, and the bedrooms also appeared to have been randomly dropped into the floor plan. It was as though a spatially challenged giant had abandoned his round of Tetris here mid-game. Clearly the place had never been meant for residential use. One could easily picture hundreds of dusty boxes full of indoor fitness apparel or stereo components lining its walls. But now Sarah and I were lining its walls, and paying an astonishing amount for the privilege.

When Sarah told me how much the room was renting for, I giggled. It was just that kind of number. You couldn't say it without giggling. Later, when Ben and Eugene asked how much I was paying, I giggled when I told them and then they giggled in response. "Oh, God," they giggled, repeating the number. "Wow. You're paying that much? For . . . this? That doesn't make any sense!" After a while, I realized that the number actually had a tonic effect on people and even considered adding it to my email signature: "My monthly rent is \$——. Have a Happy Day!" In truth, the room cost only two hundred dollars per month more than the one-bedroom apartment in Red Hook, but now instead of a furnished apartment all to myself, I was getting a bare futon in a room without a closet whose only light came from a Virgin Mary statue with a lightbulb screwed into its head. And, of course, I had a new roommate. Or rather, as I would soon learn, *roommates*.

That first evening, after I'd deposited my meager pile of books and clothes in my new bedroom, I went over to the art gallery next door. It was having an opening and Sarah had suggested we meet up there after work. I got myself a plastic cup of white wine and loitered awkwardly against a back wall, waiting for her to appear. There was a painting of a dog fucking a pig with an American flag drawn on its belly and another painting of a girl giving a clown a blow job. But mostly, I was surrounded by dozens of sketches of badly drawn penises. I don't know if it was the wine or just my frayed nerves, but as I looked around the room, the penises seemed to wobble threateningly toward me. They wagged their misshapen heads, ululating softly like some deranged Greek chorus, "Do you have any idea what you're doing here? Here in Brooklyn? Here in Williamsburg? Here on Hope Street? Any idea at all?" And then Sarah appeared in the doorway.

"Hey, you!" she called, and then waved at the room, drawing a wreath through the cigarette smoke around the pigs, the clowns, and the penises. "Don't you just *love* this?"

Sarah's old roommate, Becca, hadn't completely moved out yet, and she had invited another friend of hers to stay over too, so now there were two people staying in Sarah's room and this other girl, whose name I didn't know, sleeping on the couch. My friends giggled even more when they considered the amount I was paying to share a bathroom with three other people. But real hilarity ensued a few days later, when I began noticing swollen bites dotting my arms and legs each morning. My first thought was mosquitoes. But it was December and this was Williamsburg, not Cambodia. There was also the fact that I was getting bitten only in bed, while sleeping. So after three nights of waking up itchy, I finally stripped back the sheets and found them there: an entire village of black fleas, pogoing merrily across the futon's white surface.

After work that night, I gave Sarah the news that I had fleas.

"I guess it's not that hard to believe," she said. "You know those sheets of cardboard under the futon? Becca dragged those in from the dumpster."

The futon officially still belonged to Becca, who was leaving for California in two days, but we decided it was better to throw it out right away, before the fleas spread. Together Sarah and I dragged the futon outside to the curb, and then I went down to the Atlantic Terminal Mall to find a cheap air mattress. When I returned later that night, Becca and Sarah were both in the living room and it was clear from the chill of silence that greeted my arrival that I'd just interrupted something. As soon as I'd slipped into the room, the yelling resumed.

"And what about Terrence? Is he, like, some kind of fucking carrier too? Is that what you think? Both of us are carriers?"

Terrence was Becca's boyfriend; I had met him once. He was a typically scruffy hipster, and not a bad candidate for carrier, actually.

"I never said that you had fleas, I just said *the bed*—"

"What about her? Don't you think maybe she's the carrier?"

"Becca, I really don't—"

"Well, I want to know why you don't think it's her. I'm supposed to be your friend. I'm the one who's been living here for a year—who the fuck knows where she came from and what she brought with her?"

I stared out my lone window at the bricked-in alley and the sad, weed-filled lot beyond—a vista one might well describe as brownfieldy. I had been in Brooklyn for less than a week and now here I was, listening to two girls fighting over whether or not I had fleas and feeling nostalgic for the ghetto I never had. Still, I thought to myself, better a flea in Brooklyn than a tick in Carrboro.

"—only two days and you're already throwing my private property out in the trash."

"I know you're upset about the futon but you know you owe me a lot more than that."

"This isn't about money, it's about *respect*, Sarah, and *trust*."

"Okay. You're right. I was wrong to throw out the futon without asking. Sorry. But what's that got to do with last month's rent, or the gas—"

"This is unbe*fucking*lievable."

Then there was a BOOM! The walls shuddered once and seemed to sigh in the sudden stillness. I waited for a minute before easing open my door to find Sarah there, sitting on the couch, staring straight ahead. For the first time since we'd met, her perpetual perkiness—a quality that made you either love her or want to lace her yogurt with arsenic, depending on your disposition—had been drained away.

"Hey," she said, not looking at me. "I guess you heard all that."

"I'm really sorry, Sarah—this is my fault."

"No, it's not your fault. She owes me money for a lot of other stuff. She's just using this thing about the futon to get out of it."

"Oh," I said softly. "Well, I'm really sorry."

"When she first moved in she was really, really cool." Sarah made a limp motion with her hand. "We were friends. It's only been lately . . . since the money . . ." Then she trailed off and when she looked up I noticed that her eyes, which were very big and very blue, were filled with tears.

I didn't know what to say. We hadn't known each other long enough for fleas and tears.

"Um. Well . . . if it helps any, I would like to offer you a nobility point." This was something Josh thought up, the nobility point.

"Wh-what?"

"A nobility point. It's like, you know, when something really shitty happened, but at least you did the right thing. Becca stole your money, but you never stooped to her level. If it were me? I would have told her to go jam it straight up her ass."

Sarah blinked at me.

"So, uh, here," I added awkwardly, patting her shoulder.

"Oh," Sarah said. "Well, thanks." And then Sarah smiled. And then she laughed.

And that, I realized, was the first truly good thing to have happened since I left North Carolina.

It was a total coincidence that Sarah happened to work as a music publicist for Lea. She hadn't mentioned it in her apartment ad and I'd found out only after agreeing to rent the room. It had been two years since I'd met Lea, yet it was an encounter I still remembered vividly because it was, in every sense, a deflowering that marked the end of innocence and cleaved my life into "before" and "after" eras. This all happened back when Josh and I were still living in Hoboken, not long after I'd released my first EP, on a tiny label. At the time I was doing all I could to promote the release, playing every show that came my way, no matter how tiny or demoralizing, sending armloads of hand-addressed CD mailers to music journalists each week, usually without much response.

Around the same time I couldn't help but notice that another local singer, Lisa Cane, who'd also just released an album on a similarly tiny label, seemed to be everywhere I wasn't. Wherever my album got a blurb, she had a feature; wherever I managed a listing, she had an interview. The explanation was probably straightforward, I thought to myself. Her music must be a good deal better than mine. A freelancer for *Spin* puts her CD on the player and its sheer awesomeness blows a hole straight through the back of her head. Whereas mine? Meh. I didn't give the matter a second thought until she started scoring opening slots for major acts, often playing two to three shows back to back in Manhattan, a practice that reliably pissed off bookers and got local bands banned from clubs for stretching their draw too thin. Something was up.

Lisa Cane did not have a manager, a booking agent, or a brand-name label. She didn't dance on bar stools naked, dress up like a velociraptor, or traffic in the kinds of scatological stunts that generate instant acclaim. Nor did she have a hit song or a large, homegrown fanbase. And yet Lisa Cane was managing to take the New York City music scene by storm. Within a couple months, she'd landed a deal with one of the best indie labels in the country. A small ache opened in my chest whenever I saw her name. How was it that she'd managed to arrive on the scene so fully formed and primed for ascent, I wondered? I was jealous. But I was also curious. So I went to her website and started looking around, hoping for some clues. And after a while, I found this mysterious directive: "For more information, contact Shellac."

Shellac, I learned, was a media relations and marketing company, but I still didn't know exactly what that meant. I sent a vague note to the address listed, expressing interest in their "services," and threw in a link to some of my MP3s for good measure. A reply came the next day from someone named Suzanne. She had listened to my songs and liked what she heard. Would I be interested in coming by the office for a visit to discuss my music, and what Shellac might do for me? I agreed and we set a date.

The following week, I showed up at the front desk of their cavernous space in the Flatiron District where the ceiling fans were whirring so far overhead they may as well have been helicopter blades spotted from the Brooklyn Bridge. I was overwhelmed by the sheer real-estate-ness of the place. A young woman who looked as though she'd just stepped out of a fashion spread in *Vice* magazine darted out from behind a workstation.

"Alina? Suzanne," she said, motioning me into a nearby office. "You're in luck. Lea said she can join us."

"I'm sorry . . . who is Lea?"

"Lea founded Shellac. Let's wait to talk until she gets here."

A few minutes later, a formidable woman arrived in the doorway, announcing herself with a jangle of heavy jewelry.

"We listened to your music," Lea said, without stepping into the room. "Tell me—did Pitchfork review your EP?"

"Y-yes," I said.

"And what was your number?"

My number? No one had ever asked me for my Pitchfork score before. It was like asking someone their IQ or their cup size or the balance of their savings account. There must be a rule somewhere saying that you can't just come right out and ask someone for *their number* without exchanging bodily fluids first. I was scared. I didn't really know whether mine was a good number or a bad number, objectively speaking. The review had been pretty good. But the number? It wasn't a terrible number, for sure. Not an amazing number, perhaps, but still—

I gave Lea my number. She stood there thinking.

"Okay," she said at last, coming unstuck from the door frame, "we can talk." Then she sank into a chair and proceeded, over the course of the next hour, to explain how everything worked.

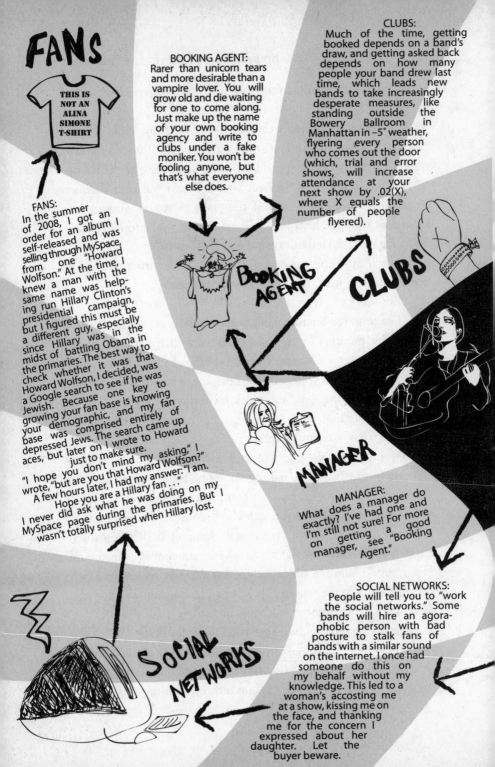

FANS

THIS IS NOT AN ALINA SIMONE T-SHIRT

FANS:
In the summer of 2008, I got an order for an album I self-released and was selling through MySpace, from one "Howard Wolfson." At the time, I knew a man with the same name was helping run Hillary Clinton's presidential campaign, but I figured this must be a different guy, especially since Hillary was in the midst of battling Obama in the primaries. The best way to check whether it was that Howard Wolfson, I decided, was a Google search to see if he was Jewish. Because one key to growing your fan base is knowing your demographic, and my fan base was comprised entirely of depressed Jews. The search came up aces, but later on I wrote to Howard just to make sure.
"I hope you don't mind my asking," I wrote, "but are you that Howard Wolfson?"
A few hours later, I had my answer: "I am. Hope you are a Hillary fan . . ."
I never did ask what he was doing on my MySpace page during the primaries. But I wasn't totally surprised when Hillary lost.

BOOKING AGENT:
Rarer than unicorn tears and more desirable than a vampire lover. You will grow old and die waiting for one to come along. Just make up the name of your own booking agency and write to clubs under a fake moniker. You won't be fooling anyone, but that's what everyone else does.

CLUBS:
Much of the time, getting booked depends on a band's draw, and getting asked back depends on how many people your band drew last time, which leads new bands to take increasingly desperate measures, like standing outside the Bowery Ballroom in Manhattan in −5° weather, flyering every person who comes out the door (which, trial and error shows, will increase attendance at your next show by .02(X), where X equals the number of people flyered).

BOOKING AGENT

CLUBS

MANAGER

MANAGER:
What does a manager do exactly? I've had one and I'm still not sure! For more on getting a good manager, see "Booking Agent."

SOCIAL NETWORKS

SOCIAL NETWORKS:
People will tell you to "work the social networks." Some bands will hire an agoraphobic person with bad posture to stalk fans of bands with a similar sound on the internet. I once had someone do this on my behalf without my knowledge. This led to a woman's accosting me at a show, kissing me on the face, and thanking me for the concern I expressed about her daughter. Let the buyer beware.

LAWYERS

LAWYERS:
Some music lawyers will shop your album to labels for a fee. Others will do it for free, on the assumption that you'll become famous one day and they'll get to negotiate your contracts. Either way, first they'll ask for a showcase. Your showcase might take place in a club or, like mine, in an office for an audience of eight guys sitting in metal folding chairs with their arms crossed.

PRESS

PRESS:
The parents of most indie rockers do not necessarily endorse their life choices. They might wish their children were pursuing a career that offered more stability, more prestige, more money. Okay, any money. It can be a thorny situation. My advice? More fame. That's right. Rather than probing wounds that have been festering for decades in therapy, devote your energy to scoring some choice press. Even a short clipping from your college alumni magazine can go a long way toward winning Mom's heart.

LABELS:
Lest one think that getting signed is the answer to all one's problems, I had a friend who got signed to a major and had to fight tooth and nail for a salary of $1,500 per month—her only source of income. That's $50 per day. Except in February, when it's $53.57 per day.

START HERE

LABELS

HELLO my name is **SUCKER**

PANDORA:
Suck up to the music curator-bots at Pandora because an editor at Farrar, Straus and Giroux might discover your music here and offer you a book deal.

PUBLICIST

PUBLICIST:
1. Some will work for anyone who pays them, even if it happens to be a Harry and the Potters cover band.
2. The best are very selective and will work your album only if they truly love it or if you are already famous. If you are unfamous, they will barter access to the well-established acts on their roster to get press for your unheard-of ass.
3. Do not be alarmed if your publicist always writes IN ALL CAPS and seems to vomit exclamation marks. It's just their way.

PANDORA

By the time Lea was done, I felt as though every song I'd ever loved, every band I'd ever worshipped, every bit of musical lore I'd ever stumbled upon and repeated was not a matter of personal taste or an act of free will, but the result of a successful campaign waged by beautifully coiffed people who moved purposefully from desk to desk in this spacious aerie with cell phones pressed to their ears.

"But I don't understand why it matters whether I send a press kit or Shellac sends it . . ."

"Because then our name is on the envelope," Lea replied briskly, "and it gets opened. People know we're selective. We're the gatekeepers—not the only ones, but one of them. Labels know we have influence, that's why they hire us."

"Is that how Lisa Cane got those great opening slots?"

"We have relationships with some of the better bookers around town. They know that if they include a band on our roster, their show will get a lot of press. When a slot opens up, they call."

My head was spinning.

"And . . . so . . . how much does all that cost?"

"It depends. There's a range." Then Lea mentioned a few of my favorite indie bands and told me their labels had kept Shellac on retainer for as long as eighteen months, easily spending tens of thousands of dollars to promote a single release.

"Well, can you . . . would you mind giving me the low end?" I asked.

Then Lea leaned forward and gave me her number. And I couldn't help it—I giggled.

I walked out of Shellac's offices that day feeling as though I'd just disembarked from the mothership onto a planet that looked very much like Earth, but was subject to completely different laws of gravity. I had always assumed that there was only one way to "make it" and that was to keep grinding your way through the club circuit until one day the right person happened to be in the room. I had really never considered that money could help lubricate the process.

Once I started keeping my ear to the ground, I found no shortage of stories. I heard about bands renting out venues themselves and booking nationally known acts just to guarantee themselves an opening slot, bands who bought up all the tickets to their own shows, then slapped "sold out" posters all over the city, bands who spent a small fortune branding themselves as the next big thing with videos and merch and tricked-out tour vans, bands who hired Shellac before they even released their first EP. All the bands I'd ever played in had done everything themselves—silkscreening posters, booking tours, writing press releases. But Shellac's roster included the kinds of bands I'd always assumed were totally DIY as well: punk bands, garage bands, Riot Grrrls, metalheads. Thus enlightened, I found it hard to go back to my old ways. The Wednesday-night gig at Bar B on the Lower East Side and the featured-performer slot at the Ristra Lounge Open Mic Night in Hoboken lost whatever luster they once had. And living with Sarah only made things worse. By week two we'd settled into a routine. She would come home from something fabulous—a sold-out show at the Bowery Ballroom, a private party sponsored by Ray-Ban, a meet-and-greet with some *Rolling Stone* journalist— breathless with the day's successes. Her client had just gotten selected for an Urban Outfitters compilation, her client was performing live on *Conan* next week, her client had just landed a profile in the *L.A. Times* . . . and on it went. I would listen to the flood of good news with a growing sense of unease. Sufficiently recovered from my trauma with the children, I had started looking for a new label again. Only this time it was considerably less easy. My leads had long since dried up. The A list had given way to the B list, and now the names of labels I was contacting read like an exotic-heirloom-seed catalogue.

"So did you reach out to anyone new today?" Sarah would ask on her way to the fridge.

"A few . . ."

"Cool. What ones?"

"Um. Thistle Heart, Unyielding Crotch, and . . . um . . . Shoot the Muffin, I think. There may have been one more."

"Oh," Sarah would say, crinkling her cute nose in confusion. Her clients were on Interscope or Matador, or some other undeniably cool and fashiony label. "I haven't heard of any of those . . . but I'm sure they're all really great! I hope one of them says yes, right?"

Then she would dash over to the CD player, yelling, "By the way, we just got this in today. It's an amazing new band from Bristol you're going to love love love!" and I would grimace as the room grew loud with bright, happy sounds.

The only way to get internet access in the apartment was to cadge it from the restaurant next door. And the only way to cadge it was by sitting on the very edge of Sarah's bed, balancing on one quarter of a butt cheek while resting a laptop on a partial slip of window ledge. I often chose to go to the coffee shop down the street instead. The music in the coffee shop was so loud that it was impossible to work, and yet every seat was always reliably full of people working. I would sit there composing sad queries to labels or following up on sad queries to labels. After two weeks of near constant effort, I'd turned up only one possibility, a small label in Acme, Michigan. They asked for a copy of the album, and as I wrote their address on a CD mailer, I wondered whether Acme was a real place. Hadn't Acme been the name of the company that manufactured the flawed contraptions in those old Road Runner cartoons? The Dehydrated Boulders and Harpoon Guns and Super Leg Vitamins that always reduced Wile E. Coyote to a tiny, smoking turd? Free association wasn't helping lift my spirits any. Especially now that it was truly winter, and Brooklyn's color-saturation knob had been dialed down to zero. One evening as I returned home after another afternoon of fruitless searching, a skinny man with an expensive haircut jogged up to me.

"Excuse me," he said. "Would you go out with my drummer?"

I stared at him. He looked sober.

"Um," I said, reshouldering my bag. "No."

"We rehearse right there," he said, pointing to a building on the corner of Roebling, as if the drummer's sheer proximity might sway me.

"Uh huh," I replied tetchily and resumed walking, picking up the pace.

"Listen. He, like, really, *really* needs to get laid," the skinny man continued sotto voce, trotting alongside me.

"Sorry to hear that." You, my friend, I thought to myself, are what make people hate Williamsburg.

"He's a totally nice guy—"

"Dude?"

"—and, to be honest? It's kind of an *emergency*."

I wheeled around to look him in the eye.

"I? . . . am married."

I'd said it and now it was very quiet. I had gotten married at twenty-five, an age by which no small number of women already have kids and mortgages as well, but here in Williamsburg, on those blocks populated mainly by rootless twentysomethings, saying "I'm married" was like announcing you were poisonous. It was like saying "I just swallowed a radioactive spider and if you stare at me for one more second, you will die too." Being married was a secret I'd kept for weeks from the first band I joined in Brooklyn, living in well-justified fear of the inevitable condemnation. A girl singer for a Brooklyn band was not supposed to be married; she was supposed to be cute and available, living a carefree life that involved drinking endless beers without ever gaining weight.

"Oh my God!" Sarah had whispered when I'd broken the news. "What's that like, being married?"

"Well, it's like . . . dating someone . . ." I'd replied slowly, careful not to scare her, ". . . only you have to, like, date that same person every day. Forever."

The man with the haircut looked at me as though a cockroach had just crawled out of my mouth.

"Oh," he said. "Shit."

And then he ran up Hope Street, in search of someone hotter and more fuckable. I made sure he had fully faded from view before turning into our doorway. Then I unlocked the metal gate and stepped onto an echoey landing full of trash bins and debris. There was a bright bar of light beneath our door and I could already hear the music blasting before I turned the knob. When I walked into the living room I found Sarah, hair tied back with a sparkly wrap, broom in hand.

"Great news," she beamed. "I found us a third roommate!"

A third roommate? But the apartment only *had* two bedrooms and weren't they both full of Sarah and me? I remember Sarah mentioning that she and Becca had once rented out the ledge on top of the bathroom cube. It was a shelf of space maybe three feet high with just enough room for a futon—ideal for vampires or people who happened to lack a torso. The girl lasted for three months before vanishing one day without a word to anyone.

"You mean for up *there*?" I asked, gesturing toward the bathroom.

"No, silly! *Here*." Sarah waved her hands vaguely at the air around us.

I scanned the room—the kitchen table? the counter? the windowsill?—and gave Sarah an uncomprehending look.

"Duh? They're going to *build* a room."

"They're going to build a room *inside* the living room? But . . . *where*?"

She walked over to the space right by the front door, the place where we flipped through the mail, the few feet we cut right across without even thinking on our way to go pee. Sarah whirled around.

"Right . . . here!" she announced.

"But that's hardly any room!"

"Well, she's only paying five hundred a month," Sarah said, shrugging a little.

"She's paying five hundred a month to live in the spot we leave our umbrellas?" I could feel the hysteria edging into my voice.

"I know, bargain, right? That girl who lived on top of the bathroom paid nine hundred. But remember, this girl has to, like, build the whole room too. And have you been to Lowe's lately? Sheetrock's *ex-peeeen-sive.*"

Sarah went off in search of a dustpan and I continued to stare at the scuffed piece of floor where she'd stood, not understanding how anyone could possibly envision a home for herself in a carpet-sized space whose only amenity was an electrical outlet. Or, for that matter, on top of a bathroom, where someone might very well be pooing right beneath her sweet ear. Yet who was I to judge? I, who slept on an air mattress in a ridiculously expensive room? I, who had only recently rid myself of fleas? Hope Street, I realized, was nothing more than a refugee camp, a tent city for the young, the poor, and the restless, the former residents of flyover states yearning to breathe free; for unwashed, muddled masses in search of opportunity, and dubious men in search of drummer concubines. The sunset gates of the Bedford Street L marked the beginning of our Camino Francés, our Santa Fe Trail, our Yellow Brick Road, and like the first settlers, we would stake our flags in dumpsters and basements, in closets big enough for a bedroll; we would float from room to room holding our laptops aloft like divining rods, in search of free signal. We would squat here until our acorns took root, until our internships bloomed into production assistantships and our air mattresses filled with down.

Like it or not: I was one of them.

The holidays were upon us and while I was fairly certain that I could handle Christmas, the approach of New Year's Eve had me considering seppuku. The day had always been an exquisite torment. I mean, was it humanly possible to have enough fun to fulfill the potential of New Year's? There would be a man in a parka on TV reporting from Times Square. In reality, he couldn't be colder if someone slipped a frozen can of Diet Coke between his balls, yet he would be smiling with all forty teeth. And he would be surrounded by a million people, all screaming ecstatically as though each and every one of them were giving birth to the Messiah right there at Forty-second Street and Broadway. I could never be this happy, and that is why I decided long ago to deliberately suck all the joy out of this holiday. I adopted a rigid routine. First there is the review of last year's resolutions, the results of which are then tabulated and ranked using an exacting scoring system. This is followed by the christening of a New Year's motto—a couplet that has to rhyme with the last digit of the forthcoming year. And finally there is the drafting of the coming year's resolutions, that delicate dance between Benjamin Franklin moral perfectionism and snarky Simon Cowell reality check. These activities leave no time for fun and require enough concentration to rule out heavy drinking, all of which is fine by me. And normally the reassuringly bureaucratic nature of these tasks is enough to blunt my New Year's anxieties. But this year was different. My only resolution had been to find a label to release my first full-length album, and there was no way around it: I'd failed. Not only that, but I was haunted by the failed resolutions and unfulfilled mottos of years past. Like how 2004 had been "The Year to Score," but I hadn't scored. And 2005 had been "The Year to Arrive," when clearly the only thing to arrive was 2006. In a last-ditch effort to salvage my year, I sent a note to the label in Acme, Michigan, to check on whether they'd had a chance to listen to my album yet. A man named Steve wrote back right away. Unfortunately, he said, the CD-R I'd burned for him had gotten stuck in his truck stereo, which now required an expensive repair. So no, he hadn't gotten around to listening yet. Happy holidays.

At least there was one thing to look forward to, and that was Josh's arrival in Brooklyn. We had been apart for only three weeks, but I had already ginned myself up to high school levels of nostalgia. And I knew Josh was anxious to see me too, mostly because my distressing little text messages (apt fell thru! i have fleas! girl 2 live in box in lvg rm!) had him concerned. Miraculously, just as he was set to arrive, we were granted a last-minute reprieve from Hope Street—our friend Eugene was going out of town with his girlfriend and offered us his cozy apartment in Park Slope. So that's where we found ourselves on New Year's Eve: planted on Eugene's couch with a romantic candle, half a bottle of wine, and a spreadsheet labeled "Resolutions2006.xls" open before us.

"You go first," I said.

"Okay. Let's see," said Josh. "I had 'The Concept of Intentional Action: A Case Study in the Uses of Folk Psychology' published in *Philosophical Studies*, and Arudra and I got 'Intention and Intentional Action: A Cross-Cultural Study' published in *Journal of Culture and Cognition*, and then that paper I wrote with your dad and Ken, 'Philosophical Implications of Inflationary Cosmology,' got accepted in the *British Journal for the Philosophy of Science*. Oh, wait, do forthcoming articles count?"

"Forthcoming is okay," I muttered.

"What about 'revise and resubmit'?"

"Fine."

In a way, I hoped that Josh's list would never end, but eventually it was my turn.

"Well," I said, in my most businesslike voice. "We all know what we know, right? I think I should just put a big double frowny face next to my New Year's resolution. And then we should make it bold. And also highlight it in red so that it really stands out." I was determined to be a man about this.

"Whoa, whoa," Josh said, clearly taken aback. "Don't you think that's a little drastic?"

"Not really."

"Well, I think you did a lot this year, you have plenty to be proud of . . . What do you say we just leave that one blank for now?"

"We can't leave it blank. This is it. The end of double oh six. The day of reckoning." My voice skipped up a register.

"How about this, let's just make it . . . let's make it a rollover resolution!"

"A *rollover resolution*?"

"Yeah. Like, we'll just put it on hold for now. Revisit it next year."

"A resolution is not like a fucking cell-phone minute, you know."

"Hey—"

"Or some kind of *Twinkie* with a thirty-year shelf life. You know what my motto for 2007 is?"

"Remember your promise—"

"Ready? Okay, here it is: 2007—Fuck it."

"Maybe we should take a break—"

"I don't want to take a break! Why is it that you *always* want to take a break? Right when things are *finally* getting interesting?

Right w-wh—" But that's when the world started spinning and I lost my train of thought.

It was the end of New Year's Eve. The next morning I woke up, aching and feverish. Weeks of camping out on the air mattress on the floor of my drafty room had finally caught up to me. But Eugene was returning home that night, so my convalescence would have to take place back on Hope Street. When we arrived, the place was empty save for the giant plywood box that stood planted in the middle of the living room. The box had only three walls and no ceiling, which meant that any box-based activities would instantly be broadcast throughout the apartment. Out of necessity, I felt that Sarah and I would have to ban the box girl from ever having sex or talking on the phone. But this conversation could wait. She wasn't moving in for another week and Sarah wouldn't be back from visiting her family on Staten Island until the next day. For now we were alone. Josh swaddled me in the two sleeping bags we used to insulate ourselves from the cold air trapped in the mattress and I spent the day in bed. The next morning I woke up, stiff and cold and snot-encrusted. Josh was already awake, peering at me anxiously.

"How are you feeling?" he asked.

"Uh, biddle bedder, I tink," I said, standing up to stretch a little. I blew my nose. Then I sniffed. From far away, I could sense a sneeze coming. I sniffed again. The sneeze blew through me, and in that moment something very bad happened. I felt eerily numb. Something—I couldn't say what—in my lower back had torqued and crumpled. A high-pitched whine erupted in both ears, like a hive of cicadas encircling my head, and blood pulsed loudly in my temples. Then, all at once, the world came crashing back in vivid Technicolor and a chasm of pain bigger than the entire state of North Carolina opened before me. In one instant, my resolutions for this year and every year thereafter were atomized and realigned. Now I had only one goal, which was to return to the pain-free existence I had blissfully enjoyed not one minute ago.

I collapsed onto the air mattress and bounced horribly on the spongy surface before coming to rest. When I hadn't moved an inch six hours later, Josh announced that he was taking me to the hospital.

"Nope."

"What do you mean 'nope'? You can't even *move*."

"I'm fine."

"We're going back to North Carolina."

"I'm not going."

"You can't stay here. This stupid air mattress is killing you—"

"It's nice. I like it."

"Look, I think—"

"Do you want to know what I think?" I interrupted.

"What?"

"*You* are not being nice."

"I just *spoon-fed you yogurt*—"

"You don't respect my autonomy."

"How can I respect your autonomy if you can't get up?"

"That's exactly what I mean."

By then Sarah had returned and she had brought her dad back to Hope Street for a visit. Josh opened the door a crack so that I could wave to him from my prone position.

"Hi, Dad!" I yelled as Josh slipped out the door to go buy me a bedpan.

But the next morning, when I hadn't moved for twenty-four hours, all resistance was gone.

"We're going home," Josh said.

"Okay," I replied meekly. "But I can't walk."

"I'll be back."

When Josh returned from the hardware store twenty minutes later, he had a four-wheel dolly with him, the kind you use to move furniture. He rolled it up to the foot of the air mattress and looked at me expectantly.

"Are you ready?"

"No," I said, holding my arms out to him.

And then, without another word, Josh hoisted me up, set me on the dolly, and wheeled me out the door.

Three weeks later I was sitting in my living room in Carrboro, on the phone with Steve from Acme, Michigan. I'd sent him another copy of my album, to replace the one that broke his car stereo. He'd written back to say he'd played it for his partner and they both liked it, but then another couple of weeks had gone by without word and, again, I'd given up hope.

"I thought it was pretty clear when we asked about your touring plans that we meant yes," Steve said.

"I guess I was just waiting for that actual word, *yes*."

"All apologies," Steve said breezily. "But you know, my partner and I are really excited about everything you guys have going down there in North Carolina."

"North Carolina?"

"Yeah, it's a great scene. Do you know Ticonderoga? They're one of our bands. From Raleigh."

I could count seven deer grazing in our backyard: four grown deer and three fawn.

"And Schooner, we're going to release their new record right before yours. A couple of those guys live in Carrboro. You're practically neighbors."

"Is that right?" I limped over to the window. They were the most beautiful things I'd ever seen.

"Yeah, you should get to know them. I keep telling my wife we should move down there. It's warm, it's cheap. And the music scene . . . I mean, what the hell is it about that place?"

Steve kept talking, and I kept gazing out at our withered lawn and the deer rooting through the long-abandoned vegetable garden, nosing the dead leaves for some fresh green shoot, hoping for an early spring.

IMAGING THE OTHER

Not long after finishing art school, I spent a few years trailing across the country after my childhood friend Amanda Palmer with a camera, documenting her life and times. It was 1999 when I embarked on the project, and back then I could have accurately been described as a young woman at loose ends. After finishing college, I worked first as a VISTA volunteer and then as a salesgirl at a toy store, before settling into the vague position of "director of special projects" for a small nonprofit. I had a lot of ideas about what I wanted to do with my life, many of which were grand and none of which stuck. I applied to programs to teach English in both Indonesia and Mexico, then declined both after getting accepted. I decided I would open a home portrait studio but did nothing more than buy a giant roll of white paper and a huge piece of black felt. I had always wanted to be a singer, so I tried busking out on Sixth Street, but then quit that too after a few weeks, when a cop told me to move along. I was not alone—I was living in slacker-era Austin, Texas, where every other person was a musician/barista/actor/minotaur.

Then there were people who seemed to be composed of nothing but the slashes themselves, like my neighbors. Most of them were on the nine-year plan at Austin Community College, and all of them kept translucent candy-colored bongs on their windowsills for easy access. They were nice people, but they did not inspire me to greater heights. Rather, they inspired me to lie down. They inspired me to play a round of air hockey, then help myself to some shrooms while listening neverendlessly to Neutral Milk Hotel and staring at some tessellated wallpaper. I started to feel like a semi on the highway that had windmilled too far in one direction; my load was starting to wobble. It had been two years since I'd finished art school, yet I had nothing to show for it. I was in danger of becoming a perennial seeker. One of those wispy women I'd taken guitar lessons from in college, who were big into yoga, had their watercolors up for sale at a local coffee shop, and always looked as though they'd stopped crying about two seconds before I walked through the door.

It turned out that I was in need of a subject at the precise moment when Amanda was in need of an acolyte. She had just returned from Germany after abandoning a language fellowship and was looking for someone to chronicle her anticipated rise from obscurity to stardom. She wanted to be photographed, so I brought my cameras and tripod to Massachusetts when I returned home for Thanksgiving. But when Amanda greeted me at the door of her apartment in Somerville—a cheerless den of bare mattresses, dirty clothes, and candlewax—I felt a twang of doubt. With the lessons of my art school education still fresh in my mind, I couldn't help but notice that she would not make an ideal subject. Unless I cut her in half and suspended her in formaldehyde, there would be no openings at White Cube. Her large-format portrait would never find its way onto the walls of a Tribeca loft or a renovated bomb shelter in Berlin. There was no chance, even, for a sidebar in *Art News*.

I knew this because I had spent much of my time in art school focused not so much on creating an original body of work as trying to puzzle out the underlying algorithm for art world success, which, as far as I could see, didn't have much to do with either talent or aesthetics. I remember one year, the winner of the highly competitive school art show was a small square of ordinary cardboard with the number 69 scrawled on it in black paint. Two other pieces popular in the student galleries at the time were a color photograph of a vulva, blown up to the size of a screen door, and a dead rat in a ziplock bag. The rat, in particular, had a way of following one around the school. I would round the corner to the darkroom only to confront it hovering at face level stapled to the wall, or turn, one hand on the door to the girl's bathroom, to feel its cloudy eyes fixed on me from some limp perch in the corner. Now, I was no Fra Angelico, but I truly believed the 69, the vulva, and the dead rat were all within safe pitching distance of even my modest talents. And yet, somehow, I knew I could never achieve the success of these innovators. There was some intrinsic quality I lacked that doomed me to my status as art school backbencher. Guts? Imagination? Self-importance? I wanted to know: What was that intangible quality that separated me from them? My portrait of Babushka cooking an egg from their dead rat?

In the photography department, this is how it went. We would gather together silently at crit to consider the glossy C print taped to the wall: a photograph of a bald man, completely naked save for a pair of bunny ears, attached to his head with duct tape, and a pair of aviator glasses. He is leaning across a credenza while a hand belonging to someone outside the frame jams what appears to be a candlestick, gently, up his ass. Light from a neon Budweiser sign on the wall gives the man's face an almost religious cast and illuminates the casual mess on the bedroom floor.

"Now *what* is it that makes us want to look at this photograph?" a professor would ask, her voice giving nothing away as her eyes made an even sweep of the room. *Damn you, cipher!* we would think to ourselves. It was a Zen koan, not a question.

"What raises this above your everyday abject scene is that Wrigley's Spearmint Gum wrapper stuck to the subject's left foot," someone would say after a respectful pause. "It's a textbook example of what Barthes would call the 'punctum' of the scene."

"The artist is, like, totally destabilizing the referent by doubling the signifiers through his interrogation of epistemologies of queerness," another of us would offer, in a well-trained voice that betrayed no doubt in whatever had just been said.

"Ultimately," a third voice would chime, "it's political."

We would discuss Lacan's mirror stage, the investigation of the apparatus, photographic specificity. Someone would bring up "issues of surveillance," or the Panopticon, or whatever. And someone else would suggest the artist was engaging in de(con)struction, using both hands to form air parentheses. A lively debate would ensue regarding whether the parentheses belonged around the (con) or the (de), but the one thing that no one would ever bring up was the fact that the man was naked, that his cock looked like the *Challenger* shuttle about to explode, and that someone was sticking something large and improbably cumbersome up his butt. And THAT, for the love of God, THAT was what made us want to look at this photograph.

After years of practicing these kinds of mental gymnastics, I figured it out. The thing that "made us want to look at this photograph" was that the subject fit into at least one of the Three Fundamental Categories. The categories weren't a required component of semiotics or art history class, yet I was convinced they were essential, as foundational to art photography as Newton's Laws were to physics, or the Four Noble Truths to Buddhism. It's just that unlike those other principles, the categories were not openly celebrated. Rather, they operated like a gnomic code, guiding us in ways we scarcely understood and dared not challenge even if we did. Of course, not everyone stayed the course. There were always exceptions, photographers so talented that they could take a picture of an orange safety cone lying on its side in an empty parking lot and it would still be worth looking at. But for the risk-averse or talent-challenged, for those of us who had no idea what we were doing in art school or were simply cynical enough to exploit the public's endless appetite for exploitation, there would always be the Three Fundamental Categories.

1. Sex and naked people

It is unsurprising that few of us would turn down a lurid peep into the lives of sex workers and porn stars. More surprising is our interest in sex amateurs and ordinary naked people, given that we know so many of them, including, on occasion, ourselves. Quite a bit of aesthetic mileage could even be gotten out of a frumpy, fully clothed person sitting at a kitchen table, so long as a dildo and a jar of K-Y Jelly lurked somewhere within the frame. Ordinary naked people could be captured dithering about in their bedrooms, at a nudist colony, or in the hospital, but the most effective tactic was to catch one in an improbable setting, like picking mushrooms in the forest, or on line at Trader Joe's. The trick was making it look natural.

2. Poor people

Poor people always make for good eye candy because their surroundings are colorfully discombobulated, shattered by some devastating war or famine, or because they are too busy dealing with the ravaging effects of drug addiction or debilitating illness to tidy up. With the exception of clean, healthy, sober poor people who nobody wants to photograph anyway, photos of the destitute were reliably more interesting than photos of the nondestitute, not only because they had tattoos or track marks or tribal scars or missing limbs, but because the faces of the poor were etched with the deep lines caused by witnessing so many unspeakable things.

3. Fat people

This is an ingenious catch-all category. It turns out that so long as a person is very, very fat, they can be photographed doing any old boring thing and people will still find it interesting. Art cognoscenti will rhapsodize about the "sculptural qualities of the flesh," or claim it has something to do with "hyperpersonal cartographies of the body" . . . but secretly? Their fetish for fat porn is just the same as everyone else's, the reason we have reality shows like *Too Big to Walk?*, *More to Love*, and *Flab to Fab*. Soon there will be a show called *Power Ass* that just puts power tools in the hands of obese contestants so that we can watch their flesh jiggle hypnotically as they compete to melt pounds away.

Of course, the Holy Grail was a subject who fit into two or more of these categories. The question was: Could you talk that obese friend of yours into a monokini? Then could you coax her into a room to pose against some mundane wallpaper, holding a poignantly commonplace object, say a watering can or maybe a desk lamp? Now let's consider the Togolese prostitute whose trust you so painstakingly earned—might he also be a war-torn refugee? Has he considered selling his spleen for food? Would he be interested in having a visual record of that transaction?

From my perspective, though—and regardless of how ultimately lucrative it might be—going off in search of an impoverished tribe of oversized horny people sounded very draining. True, Amanda did not fit into one of the Three Fundamental Categories, but I was lazy, and it was easier to just stay put and document the life of a friend I'd had since middle school. Plus, by doing so, I could adopt a conveniently sanctimonious attitude, turning up my nose at those who preyed on the fat, the unclothed, and the financially challenged, because I was not "imaging the other," I was imaging someone just like me.

Which isn't to say that Amanda was normal. She had purple hair, feigned a British accent, and liked to wander around Cambridge in a cape. In fair weather, she could reliably be found standing on a milk crate in Harvard Square dressed in an old wedding gown and black wig, her face shellacked behind a thick layer of Jack Stein Theatrical Pancake Stage Make-up. This was how she paid her rent, working as a street performer, a human statue she named "The Eight Foot Bride." She would stand there motionless until someone dropped some money into the tin cup at her feet. Then the Bride would come to life, fluttering her eyes, gracefully rearranging her arms, blowing an air kiss in slow motion, like some ghostly drowned Ophelia.

But the singular characteristic that I found most fascinating about Amanda was her bald determination to become famous. It was an ambition I first observed in eighth grade, when Amanda cast me in the supporting role for a musical she'd written called *On Their Own*, an *Annie*-meets–*Les Miserables* mash-up about a gang of sixth-grade girls who run away to the Big City. Spurred on by their charismatic ringleader, Wanda, the girls take over an abandoned alleyway and build a fort out of plywood scraps where they spend a long time discussing how lonely and misunderstood they feel. Eventually they run out of provisions and come to realize there is no place like home, but unfortunately not before singing songs like "Build This House," "Together Forever," and the Are-You-There-God-It's-Me-Margaret-ish "If You're Up There." There were maybe five of us girls, and we would meet after school in the parlor of the sprawling Victorian where Amanda's family lived. I remember struggling to follow along on my dense lyric sheet as Amanda led us through our numbers at the piano, feeling more than a bit dazzled, even then, by her seriousness and discipline.

The truth was, I always wanted what Amanda had, and thought that maybe by keeping close and watching carefully, I could get it too. I coveted her confidence, her clarity of purpose, her indifference to what everyone else thought, and her ability to voice her most grandiose desires with neither embarrassment nor self-doubt. I coveted those qualities of hers because secretly I had the same dreams of self-fulfillment, adventure, a life of my own making. I too wanted to be adored. But the difference was that, like most people, I wanted those things only from that safe perch on the ledge of my own imagination. I wasn't interested in hustling for whatever opportunity might help get my foot in the door out in the real world. Not like Amanda. Amanda was more than willing to make the requisite sacrifices. She would happily drive her hard nail of talent into the soft underbelly of the music industry while the rest of us stood around polishing our turds, sucking our lattes, and cursing the minutes lost switching between Word and Internet Explorer. So if I couldn't be her, I figured I could at least see how it was done, from the front row, with one eye to the viewfinder.

But it did not take long for me to realize how elusive a quality Amanda's ambition was to capture in a still photograph. All the viewer ever saw was a young woman eating a bagel or sitting on a folding chair and talking on the phone. They didn't see the patina of poignancy that Amanda's youthful dreams cast over the scene. They had no way of knowing that this young woman was a precelebrity, and her half-eaten bagel and telephone would soon be available on eBay. *Or* that she was tragically fated never to become famous. That she would end up on the street, unironically clutching a paper cup that said "Have a Happy Day," begging for change in Harvard Square and mourning the halcyon days of bagels and telephones.

The people photographing fat men making toast did not have this problem. That's because theirs was not a nuanced story of a young woman at the crossroads of fate and desire, but an unambiguous story of fat men making toast. To understand Amanda, I decided, the viewer needed more context. And so I switched to videotape, which I quickly found had a lot of advantages. With a video camera in my hand, my information-gathering powers broadened considerably. I could ask a million different questions, breaking Amanda's ambition down into its molecular components. I could grind away at the witnesses, her family and friends, her bandmates and lovers, until I came to understand the source of her confidence. And in the end, I would be able to gather all that evidence, those endless miles of footage, and from the safety of a darkened room, study it until the answer revealed itself—the secret ingredient, the Three Fundamental Categories, the Four Noble Truths, the twelve-step plan—whatever thing it was that made success finally possible.

As it turned out, I didn't watch the tapes for nine years. I transferred all the Hi-8 tapes to VHS for easy viewing, then put them in a cardboard box, stuck them in a broom closet, and forgot about them. When I finally did decide to watch them, it wasn't because I was looking for a primer on how to get famous; it was because my back went out and I couldn't do much else. It happened one day after the cat threw up on the rug. I had washed it as best I could in the bathtub and then laid it out on the balcony to dry. But as luck would have it, the next day it rained, and it continued to rain for two weeks straight. The rug developed a fungus, a cheerful, cotton candy looking thing that raced along the rug's edges. It looked too happy to be there to go away without a fight. I decided to throw the whole thing away, but didn't figure on how heavy the waterlogged rug would be when I bent down to pick it up. That's how my back went out and that's when I remembered the tapes.

I shuffled into the living room and slipped the first VHS tape into the player. I was eating a yogurt—an activity that mercifully required no back muscles—and the cat jumped up onto the coffee table, politely drilling me with his stare. The cat was fat and I wasn't supposed to give him any yogurt. He kept staring. I gave him some yogurt. The cat went cross-eyed with pleasure. And the tape began.

I was back in Lexington with Amanda again, in the passenger seat of her old silver station wagon. It was autumn and brilliant-colored leaves swirled across the lawns like scratch tickets blowing through a Shell station.

"Should we start in chronological order?" I am asking Amanda, who for some reason is wearing a wreath of tinfoil stars in her hair.

"No, there's too much," Amanda says. "We should pick a few choice sites. Let's see . . . there's the bridge above Grant Street and the story of Randy Jeffries, there's the Hastings grave where I broke up with Jason, and then there's the bungalow by Granny Pond where I gave my first blow job, but I didn't know how, so it wasn't a real blow job . . ."

"More like a tentative licking?" I supplied.

"Yes," she agreed, nodding. "More a tentative licking."

We needed some heartbreakingly raw footage of Amanda recalling her tawdry upbringing on the streets of Lexington to juxtapose against all the footage that would come later, the postfame footage. I had decided it was better to tape it now, before the Givenchy ads and charity telethons, the plastic surgeries, addiction to prescription painkillers, and botched third-world adoption schemes. Yes, better now, while Amanda was still relatively fresh-faced and unself-conscious. I had planned to intercut this footage with another interview, where I'd asked Amanda to describe Lexington, the colonial town where we'd both grown up, for someone who'd never been there before.

"Lexington is *so safe*. It's the *safest place in the world*," Amanda exhaled heavily before continuing in a sing-song voice. "You can leave your bike out on the lawn, you don't really have to lock your house. It is so clean and so well manicured and the *people* there are so well manicured. They all have a prop. Whether it's their baby carriage prop, or their newspaper prop, or their intellectual book prop. They all convene at Starbucks and they all order triple short lattes with a shot of hazelnut and no whipped cream and low-fat milk. And they say it *so quickly*. It arrives in their cup and they pay their four dollars and they walk out into the sun and they sit on a bench and they watch their neighbors go by and they smile and wave and the dogs stop to sniff at each other's asses. *And everything is perfect*. Not a thing is amiss, not even the little punk kids in their little punk clothes that cost them lots of money, also sitting outside of Starbucks talking about how *fucked up* Lexington is and how *fucked up* the world is."

Then I remember the dilemma that Amanda faced growing up in Lexington, once the site of revolutionary bloodshed, now the site of Philip Ciampa Salon & Day Spa, Evolve Pilates, and La Riviera Gourmet. She wanted trouble—the one commodity in short supply. The year I graduated from high school, a woman who lived out on Ridge Road was stabbed in her home and ended up bleeding to death because the guy on duty at the local fire department assumed that hers was a prank call. Which is just another way of saying that Amanda had her work cut out for her when she launched her own private war of independence. She was arrested at fifteen for shoplifting, the same year that she had an affair with her thirty-five-year-old piano teacher. But these were run-of-the-mill transgressions, the stuff of after-school specials. By graduation she had perfected the art of being a fuckup, attracting police attention for stunts like crashing Lexington's legendary Patriot's Day parade with a group of friends dressed in tutus and ski goggles calling themselves the Scottish Socialist Tea Party. Myself, I'd always been jealous of the simple fact that Amanda managed to get out of taking *math* in high school. "It just wasn't going to happen," she'd replied briskly when I asked her about it once. This was something I'm sure I could never have accomplished, not if I'd shown up at school with a harpoon sticking out of my eye.

We drive to the bridge above Grant Street where her parents once caught her making out with a "wayward" youth, really just a kid from our high school who lived on welfare with his mom in the Battle Green Inn. We stop at Dunkin Donuts for coffee because it is not Starbucks, and then continue on to Battle Green Square, which might best be described as New England's most historic traffic island. I train the camera on Amanda as she climbs up onto the Minuteman statue and spends a good minute up there groping the Minuteman's crotch.

"I always thought he had the best ass ever of anyone in the world," she calls out, slipping back to the ground. "It's, like, so perfect and rounded and firm, you know?" Without a beat, she turns to point at a stately brick Colonial across the street. "That's the rectory of the church I went to. I should totally take you there."

But unsurprisingly, we head in the opposite direction from the church, over to the Old Belfry, where Amanda smoked her first cigarette. Then we drive to the site of the aborted blow job, a little stone bench nestled in a patch of woods that happened to be located on someone's private property. There, Amanda tells me how it ended, with Peter Tortelli zipping up his pants and refusing to ever speak to her again, even after she sent him the lyrics to "The Same Deep Waters as You" by the Cure, painstakingly written out in longhand on romantic paper. We make our way back to the main road. New England autumn, at its tourist-trapping peak, explodes all around us. The camera shakes as I follow Amanda out of the woods, back to her car. And that's where the footage suddenly breaks off. There is some static, and when the picture comes back into focus she is gone and suddenly I am back in the kitchen of my parents' house, where I find them arguing over a casserole.

I was sorting through the tapes, looking for another good bit to watch and remembering that the road to fame was a twisty one, and there was a time when Amanda, like me, was all talk and little traction. She would wax on about writing songs, forming a band, playing shows, getting famous . . . but whenever I checked in, she wasn't doing any of these things. What she was doing was falling into bed with guys she happened to sit next to at Café Pamplona and standing on a milk crate in Harvard Square while tourists took her picture for a dollar. Maybe this is why we came up with the idea of the road trips—because aside from shooting Amanda performing as the Eight Foot Bride or mooning around coffee shops, there wasn't much of a story here.

But there must have been some deeper explanation for why we decided to drive aimlessly around the country for weeks, video-taping the Eight Foot Bride in a series of increasingly improbable locales. My loneliness? Her desperation? A mutual desire to live out some kind of Jack Kerouac, *On the Road* fantasy? The tapes were poorly labeled, though, so I managed to find only one other clue, from the night we spent in a trashy motel near Niagara Falls. We had gone to a strip club downtown earlier that evening, where Amanda had kissed me. She did it right there at the table as we were nursing our watery cocktails and watching a Chippendale's wannabe grope a drunk Buffalo housewife on her birthday. It was the first time I'd ever kissed a girl, but after a few days of life on the road with Amanda, such things had come to seem normal. It would have been more shocking, I think, had we just watched some *Full House* reruns and gone to bed early. Anyway, we returned to our motel room, where a photo mural of an island paradise was fighting a losing battle with the very real landscape of urban decay just outside our window. Amanda dumped half a bottle of bubble bath into our heart-shaped Jacuzzi and let the hot water run. When the tub was full, she crawled in. I am off to the side somewhere, as usual, taping.

"Why are we here?" I ask her. "What is the purpose of this trip?"

Amanda leans against the red plastic lip of the tub, arms akimbo and pit hair in full bloom. A delta of black mascara has formed beneath each eye. There is a pause. And then she shrugs.

"I just love the idea of putting things where they don't belong."

I was one of those things, I thought to myself. The less-

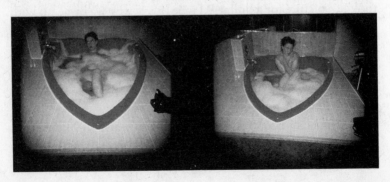

glamorous hanger-on. I had been twenty pounds heavier back then and now cringed whenever I saw myself on tape. I hit fast-forward and watched Amanda watching rainbows suspended in the mist of Niagara Falls until the tape ended. There were other questions that I wanted answered, but the tapes defied any kind of logic. Whenever I cued up a new one, it invariably started in the middle, in some weird and disorienting new place. Like this scene, here, where I am crashing over a carpet of dead leaves, then stopping to zoom in on a hand-painted sign that reads: IN BAD WEATHER, STUMP SERVICE WILL BE HELD IN THE AUDITORIUM. We were in Lily Dale, a small community in upstate New York that was home to the world's largest community of "Spiritual-ists," tromping through a pet cemetery, looking for a good place for Amanda to set up the Eight Foot Bride.

"We haven't gone to the Healing Tree yet, have we?" I call ahead to Amanda.

"No," she shouts back over her shoulder.

Amanda is dressed like a trick-or-treater minus the paper bag, in a shiny purple cape with leopard-print trim. By the time we arrive at the Forest Temple, it is too late. The sun is setting through the trees and there isn't enough light left to shoot. So we get back in the car and then drive to Cleveland. We sleep in Amanda's station wagon, in the parking lot of a Days Inn, and set off to try our luck again in the morning. Time jerks ahead. We are pulling into the tranquil landscaped grounds of the Our Lady of Lourdes Shrine and Grotto in Euclid, Ohio, with Swollen Members' "Paranoia" blasting through our open win-dows. Amanda turns to flash a crooked smile at my ever-ready Hi-8 cam and then slows to give a nearby statue of Jesus a jaunty thumbs-up. We pause to make an offering of fifty cents at the grotto altar. Good insurance, I suppose, considering what was to come.

No, I thought, as I watched myself loudly debating the pluses and minuses of various camera angles with Amanda, pointing first at the stone-faced grotto, then at a row of nearby pews. *No!* But yes, in the next shot there is Amanda, emerging from the backseat of the Volvo in her wedding dress, black wig slightly askew. She checks her makeup in the window of the station wagon one last time before grabbing the milk crate and setting off for the shrine, a dirty bride's veil trailing several feet behind her. Amanda sets up in front of the statue of the Blessed Mother, at the base of the grotto. The words "I am the Immaculate Conception" hover above her head in a gold halo. She gets up on her milk crate, bows her head, and assumes a prayerful pose. *What is wrong with you?* I screamed silently at myself. *Put that fucking tripod away!* The shrine was not only a site of religious pilgrimage, it was also home to an order of nuns, the Sisters of the Most Holy Trinity. Did we ever stop to think what might happen if one of them chanced by and found us there? But I had a feeling that even if John the Baptist himself had dropped in for a flagon of holy water, in our supreme arrogance we wouldn't have stopped filming.

We kept pressing west, putting things where they didn't belong. There is the Eight Foot Bride, blending in as one of the ears in

a field of concrete corn sculptures in Dublin, Ohio; in a forest in Hell, Michigan; wedged between a griffin and a white-robed goddess at the Lawn Ornament Capital of the World in Lenox, Michigan; standing on the dusty floor of an abandoned farmhouse we find off the highway somewhere in Illinois. The cops finally catch up with us in Indiana, where we are filming Amanda on the railroad tracks running alongside I-65. Someone had called the police from their cell phone to report that a bride was trying to commit suicide. They laugh at us and let us go, and when the footage starts up again, I have no idea where we are.

The opening shot is a shaky close-up of a cup filled with what looks like dirty bong water. It turns out to be coffee. We are at a diner eating breakfast and yet it is clearly nighttime, the sky outside the windows is dark, punctuated only by the acid glow of distant streetlamps. Wan plants dangle from the acoustic ceiling tiles. The table is covered with loads of food—home fries and eggs under a layer of cheese that looks as natural as vinyl flooring. We are salting it liberally. A man with close-cropped hair sits across from us. His arms are covered in tattoos and he is wearing a crucifix over a sweatshirt that says FLORIDA in big red letters. But I know we are not in Florida either.

"Why are you here and where are you going and who are you?" the man is asking Amanda.

"Thas sree quessions," Amanda says through a mouthful of potatoes. "Ass one."

"Okay," the man says. "I'll ask the most important one. Who are you?"

Now I remembered. The car had broken down. We were in the Midwest somewhere. We'd gone looking for a mechanic earlier, but couldn't find one and had to wait until morning.

"I'm Amanda Palmer," Amanda says, and then adds, smiling through her food, "Narcissist."

But I must have filmed something besides this march of determined weirdness: Amanda as the Eight Foot Bride on the balcony of a castle made of tinfoil in Florida, Amanda's veil illuminated in the ghastly half-light of an underpass in Montreal, Amanda bisecting the O of a giant illuminated sign spelling HOPE on the lawn of a suburban church in Michigan. I recalled that vague period of time between our first road trip and our second, when Amanda suddenly started taking songwriting more seriously. There were fewer dreamy walks spent airbrushing the days of some ill-defined future. Now the talk was of concrete plans. The band she was forming. The shows she was playing.

I searched through the box of tapes until the dust made my fingers itch, but I found what I was looking for. We are back in the parlor of Amanda's parents' house in Lexington, and I am facing Amanda at the piano, in the same spot where I sat through countless rehearsals of *On Their Own*. A year has passed since our first road trip. Now Amanda is living in a low-rent artists' complex called the Cloud Club and she's started playing shows at the smaller clubs around Cambridge. During that same span of time, I had gotten a second cat and continued working as the director of special projects. Amanda wants to play me a new song she just wrote that she's clearly excited about. I must have come over first thing in the morning, because her purple hair is mussed and she is wearing a t-shirt and shorts that look slept in. Soon she is hitting the keys so hard that every note is accompanied by the heavy *klung* of ivory slamming wood. The veins in Amanda's neck are bulging and her gaze is turned inward. It's a good song, but I don't seem to be listening. Or maybe the spectacle makes me uncomfortable. Either way, the camera drifts away. It spends a while bobbing around the room like a drunk mosquito, before finally coming to rest on a light fixture overhead, where it stays until the end of the song.

And then there is some footage of one of Amanda's first

shows. I recognize the place. We're at Zeitgeist, a tiny art gallery that used to be two blocks from my grandmother's apartment. The place has been shuttered for years, plywood nailed over the windows and painted black. I still drive by it every time I go home to visit. Amanda is dressed up like a Claymation figure from a Tim Burton movie, with black curlicues painted around her eyes in a spidery hand. The cellist that she may or may not still have been sleeping with at that point is on stage too, his hair in pigtails. There are maybe ten of us in the audience, arranged on a smattering of folding chairs, but from the way Amanda carries herself, you'd think this is Madison Square Garden. Everything about the way she moves—the exaggerated arc of her wrist hovering above the keyboard, a single finger dropping to a high C like a hungry bird plunging into water—has a mysterious weight to it that commands attention. But because the gallery is completely dark I have the camera in night-vision mode, which turns Amanda an unfortunate shade of radioactive green and her eyes into zombified laser beams. Also distracting were the two friends I'd brought with me, people who wouldn't have enjoyed this kind of music under the best of circumstances and could barely contain their eye-rolling. As soon as we are back out on the sidewalk one of them turns to me, pushing his big green face into the camera.

"That SUCKED!" he yells. And then there is just the sound of my laughter, echoing greenly down the empty street.

Finally there is this, an interview on a beach somewhere on the southeastern seaboard. Amanda has just returned from peeing in the ocean and now we are lying down on the sand, where she shades her eyes from the midday sun, framed by the wind-whipped ocean and a shore drained of color. We are talking about work.

"What do you say when people ask you what you do?" my disembodied voice asks from behind the camera.

"The answer really depends on who's asking me. Generally I tell them that I'm a mime for a living, but I'm really just supporting myself as a musician with street theater."

"You seem so immune from the outward pressure to get a normal job. Could you talk more about that?"

"I'm just against doing something for someone else for money that I don't care about—I think most people are. I don't think that's so strange."

"But *most* people do it . . ." I prod.

"I don't want to get down on people," Amanda begins, shifting to one elbow, "but I think there are hundreds of creative ways to make money and people are just not into exploring them. I like not having to depend on anyone. You are totally responsible. If it fails, it fails—and that's fine. You do what you want to do. If you want to make X amount of money you obviously have to put in X amount of effort, and I like things that way. It's simple. I can't imagine how frustrating it is to be working in an office and be totally productive or nonproductive and still get your twelve-fifty an hour. That must feel *fucking awful*."

Twelve-fifty an hour, at the time, was fifty cents more than I was making directing special projects—none of them my own. And the thing Amanda didn't realize was that the frustrated office people, the ones not exploring making money in nonconventional ways, the ones feeling fucking awful, were me. And the thing I didn't realize at that moment, lying on the beach, was that the conversation I was having with Amanda was actually a conversation I was having with myself. It *did* sound so simple when Amanda put things that way. Knowing what you want and then doing it. Cause and effect. Effort equals outcome. Then what was it that stopped me from even trying?

"So what would your ideal job be?" I hear myself ask in a strained voice.

"I'd like to make my money putting out CDs and touring," Amanda replies in the same even tone. "The ultimate goal is to become an icon . . . I don't really even have to be *famous* famous. I wouldn't even mind being a small-time icon, as long as I was a little icon somewhere. I would like 'Amanda Palmer' to be indicative of something." She stares up at the sky for a moment, then adds, "That would be nice."

"Why do you want that?" I sputter. "I mean, it just seems so . . . so . . . outwardly focused."

"Well you *asked* me how I wanted to make my living," says Amanda, still nonplussed. "I mean, that's not *all* I want out of life. I'd just rather make my living that way than doing street theater."

"But . . . okay, let's talk about the icon thing . . . It seems like you want to capitalize on this narcissistic aspect of yourself—"

"Yes, but I think it's possible to be an icon and not just be an attention-grabbing fuck. The way I've noticed things work, even on a small scale, is there's just certain people that like having that . . . that experience. Just experiencing someone who is singing and dancing. And there are no hidden agendas in that if you get it right. I have my own very, very small little core of fans who like what I do. They just like to watch me. Even when I'm not playing the piano—they think that my life is neat and exciting, and even if they have their own neat and exciting lives, they like to follow mine, they get off on it. And I get off on them getting off on it. It's not a situation where I'm demanding their attention, I just know they like to watch me and I like to perform and there's a nice little synchronicity there. And I think that could work on a larger scale for everybody's benefit, not just mine." And with that Amanda calmly excuses herself to go put on some more sunscreen and I start fidgeting angrily with the camera controls, turning her into a pastel cartoon.

What was extraordinary to me about this scene, nine years later, was not how bitter and lost and full of schadenfreude I was—I already knew this about myself, perhaps even then—but how perfectly Amanda predicted her own future. Our conversation on the beach took place years before she started her band, the Dresden Dolls, before they signed to a major label and toured with Nine Inch Nails, before she sold a couple hundred thousand albums and played sold-out solo shows from Sydney to Japan to London, before she created an original play for the American Repertory Theater, performed with the Boston Pops, published two books, or amassed so many fans that she could earn $19,000 in ten hours by sitting on her sofa and auctioning off her stockings, her glass dildo, her ukulele, and her empty wine bottles online. And yet, even back then, before any of that, she still *knew*. Regardless of whatever else was going on, in a tutu or a torn wedding gown, from the balcony of a tinfoil palace or deep in the forests of Hell, she already had the answer to those three fundamental questions, the ones some nameless man in some placeless place is always there to ask: Who are you? Where are you going? And why are you here?

I don't have the tape from the last time I filmed Amanda, because there is no tape. A heavy hand on my shoulder stopped me before I could even start filming. I was living in Hoboken then and the Dresden Dolls were playing their first show on the main stage of the Knitting Factory in Manhattan. The show was starting in just a few minutes and I was in the middle of adjusting my tripod when the bouncer interrupted me.

"Sorry, you can't film in here," he said, putting a hand in front of the lens.

"Oh, don't worry—she's a friend of mine." I smiled. "I have Amanda's permission." I had to stare up at the man as I said this—he was mountainous.

"I don't think you understand," the bouncer continued without removing his hand. "You don't have prior authorization to shoot in here."

"Look"—I turned around and started motioning frantically to Amanda up onstage—"we can clear this up in a minute. I'll just get Amanda and she'll tell you—"

"I'm afraid I can't have you hassling the artist with the show about to start. Now I'm gonna ask you one last time: put that camera away or you'll have to leave."

That night I went home, drew a hot bath for myself, got in it, and cried. I knew it was time to quit. Amanda belonged to the world now and there would be many other people on hand to document the rest of her story, the famous part. But that's not what made me cry. What made me cry was that even though I had all the tapes, I was no closer to the answer. And I still wanted what she had.

Our last road trip ended in Key West, where Amanda wanted to spend a few days sucking money from the heavy foot traffic in Mallory Square. There is the Eight Foot Bride, aloft on a milk crate that is carefully swathed in white gauze and fake lace. She is standing tall with her arms frozen, extended upward toward the night sky. But something about the picture seemed wrong. I looked closer and realized what it was: beneath the veil, the black wig, and the white face paint, it's not Amanda's face. It's mine. I remember now: she'd talked me into it, into dressing up as the Eight Foot Bride on our last night in Key West. We decided it would be good for me, after all these years of filming, to see what it was like to be Amanda from the inside. Now I'm staring at my younger self and yet the face I see remains inscrutable. It's not me and it's not Amanda—it's just the Eight Foot Bride. She is wearing a mysterious smile and gazing out at some indefinite point, pinned against an unfamiliar backdrop of swaying palms. And I can't help but wonder what it is she sees out there. And what she can possibly be thinking as she stands frozen, waiting for a passerby to finally break the spell that brings her back to life by throwing a dollar at her feet.

I WANTED UNICORNS

A few years ago, I was baptized by a renegade priest into an unrecognized offshoot of the Russian Orthodox Church. I did not tell anyone and started off the morning of my baptism with a lie to my cousin's girlfriend regarding exactly where I was going and why it was that no, I couldn't have any kasha or even a cup of tea first. I left her concrete high-rise in St. Petersburg, the same as any other in Russia, at an early hour with nothing but a hair dryer, a pair of clean underwear, and a white cotton dress in a black plastic bag.

The Punk Monk met me outside. He was dressed in his usual outfit of black jeans and a sweater. Taken together with his long, tangled beard and sunken blue eyes, he could have been mistaken for an extra from the cast of *Harry Potter and the Goblet of Fire*. We went around to the back of the building, to a dirty footpath that cut through a series of gray towers. I was dying of thirst. The Punk Monk had told me that I had to fast for my baptism— no food or water after midnight—but he had forgotten to warn me against imbibing vast quantities of wasabi and soy sauce right up until 11:59. All night I had lain awake on Tanya's sofa, dreaming of a cool glass of St. Petersburg tap water with its sweet, bowel-melting parasites. Now, as we walked, I greedily considered the snowmelt—grimy from the soles of hundreds of feet and the gray fog of exhaust, true, but cold and refreshing nonetheless.

We reached a thoroughfare and picked our way along the side of a road that had no sidewalk. Did I have the dress? the Punk Monk asked. Yes, I replied. I'd bought it yesterday after giving my great-uncle Oleg the slip in downtown St. Petersburg. I pulled out the dress, a thing so sexless it could have been mistaken for a laundry bag, and showed it to the Punk Monk, who nodded his approval. Did I manage to find an English translation of the Nicene Creed? Yes, and here was the printout I'd made from the internet while Tanya was in the bathroom. No food or water, right? Right, I said, though I had to confess, I was considering lying down in the gutter and interrupting the rushing sludge with my face at that very moment. The Punk Monk did his best to console me with the thought that a few hours from now I would enjoy a tiny sip of wine as part of the ceremony. One last thing, he asked: How was my Church Slavonic? Would I be able to read the prayers by myself? We were marooned on a traffic island, on a street that seemed to lack any signals or signs, buffeted by the vacuuming sound of passing traffic. I squinted up at him.

"My Church Slavonic is . . . bad," I said. In all truth, my Church Slavonic did not exist.

"It's okay," said the Punk Monk, sensing my anxiety. "We'll figure something out."

I grasped for the proper etiquette, the right thing to say as you walk to church with a monk, on the way to your own baptism. Had it been a glorious day, I suppose I could have praised God for it and pointed out a blooming field of lilacs nearby, or a duck giving birth. As it was, the weather was foul and the setting an ugly, congested strip on the northern outskirts of St. Petersburg, just past the point where the subway gives up and dies. So I was grateful when the Punk Monk interrupted the silence to ask what I did last night, and I could tell him all about the Auktyon concert I'd gone to with my cousin Kolya at a place called The Place. Auktyon was a legendary St. Petersburg band, one that got its start in the glory days of the Soviet rock underground.

"Yeah, they're too 'artistic' for me," the Punk Monk said. He held me back with one arm as a dirty bus skimmed the curb. "Since the Silver Age, poets in Russia have been considered almost like secular priests, teachers of life. And Russian rock, as a descendant of Russian poetry, resumed in this tradition. But not Auktyon—I am afraid they are simply too intellectual."

I didn't understand what the Silver Age had to do with anything, or why Auktyon had to be "secular priests." Couldn't they just be a good band?

"I don't think you're being fair," I said. Now we were crossing the street, forging our way through an unplowed parking lot.

"I do respect them," said the Punk Monk.

"Have you even seen them live? I've never seen a better live show in my life. Maybe *you're* the one who's too intellectual." Dimly I realized that I was yelling, that I had stopped in a puddle and icy water was sinking into my boots.

The Punk Monk had stopped too, but he merely looked past me and raised his hand. A car glided to a stop some feet in front of us.

"I'm afraid it's going to take us too long to walk," he said. "And I have to do a funeral at eleven. We'd better hurry."

Mine, I must admit, was a weak-ass conversion. I was an amateur, my conviction nothing more than the accrual of semisober revelations that struck late at night, in the back booths of bars in faraway cities. When the Punk Monk found me, it was two years into my experiment of ditching any real career prospects for a life of crooning sad songs in the clubs, watering holes, and

DIY venues that made up the indie-rock circuit. I toured my way through an endless blur of record stores, house shows, vegetarian cafés, radio stations, strip malls, bookstores, and cavernous, echoingly empty clubs, drinking gas-station coffee, sleeping on couches, and singing the same songs in a different city every night. The pay was fifty dollars, or a compliment from the sound guy, or nothing at all. The thing that drove me to do this was impossible to resist, the closest I'd ever come to any kind of "calling," but day-to-day, it was a rootless and repetitive grind. Mostly, I drove and I begged: begged clubs to let me play, begged people to buy a CD, begged newspapers for a listing. Rinse, wash, repeat. The highs from any given success wore off after half an hour, but the lows would level me for weeks. There were no guarantees—you could throw years into the slot machine of life this way and still come up with nothing—and I was full of what-ifs, always second-guessing. It was only a matter of time before I fell victim to the clichéd consequences of prolonged introspection. I mean, when you are sucking a gin and tonic through a stirrer straw at three in the afternoon in a saloon in Battle Creek, Michigan, waiting for your sound check, and listening to a man at the bar beg a woman to have a peek at her breast cancer surgery scar, the questions "Why am I here?" and "What does this all mean?" are very good questions indeed.

My friend Konst once told me that the acoustics in the baptismal font were the most amazing thing he'd ever heard and that's what started it.

"Everything sounded so strange, so beautiful," he'd said.

"Were you in some kind of pond?" I'd asked. Konst was not a small man.

"No, a big tub. Nothing I could really swim around in. More like a vat."

He had converted to Russian Orthodoxy after college, feeling rudderless, trying to avoid a quarter-life crisis.

"It was fucking great under there. I didn't want to get out."

"And then what happened?"

"Well, I got out, eventually."

"And . . . ?"

"And I felt great."

I was jealous. An image formed right then in the back of my mind, of me floating in that warm and blissful dark, hair billowing upward, a sacred jellyfish, quietly humming. I knew it was wrong to eye the baptismal font like a kid eyeing the ball pit at Chuck E. Cheese, but the urge wouldn't go away. When I encountered the Punk Monk, years later, it was my first thought. That he must have one of those giant vats stored away somewhere, that he could do this for me.

We met through music, because we were both fans of the Soviet punk singer Yanka Dyagileva. Obsessed, actually. Yanka's albums were the soundtrack for all my ceaseless travel. I drove through America alone, listening to her albums for hours, singing along without really understanding the words. The songs were beaten out quickly on out-of-tune guitars, her voice so raw and unadorned it felt like a claw hammer tunneling its way directly into my heart. It was the sound of pain and sorrow and it had a way of fusing with the landscape, lending everything its dark, passion-filled hue. When Yanka sang "On a parallel track, a black satellite flies. It will calm us and save us and bring us peace," the world outside my windshield reverberated with symbolic significance. The Waffle Hut. The suspension tower. The odd, lunglike pieces of car littering the road. I would sing myself hoarse driving west on I-80, tears streaming down my face, ginning up my sorrow, wallowing in it.

For a long time, I knew only two things about Yanka's life: that she was from Siberia and that she drowned when she was twenty-four years old. Then I started to do some research. Her career began in 1987; it ended four short years later. Mostly, she recorded her songs live, no overdubs, no effects. She did not wear makeup. She did not dance. She refused to give interviews. In the Soviet Union, Yanka's career had no precedent. Soviet women all worked at some boring institute. They married young and had kids right away. They did not wear combat boots. They did not listen to the Velvet Underground and crisscross the country by train to give living-room concerts in the apartments of strangers. I wondered how it was that Yanka avoided whatever mysterious initiation process must occur sometime during high school, when Russian women are taught to tweeze their eyebrows to the width of a quark. I had grown up Russian American, five thousand miles away, in much easier circumstances, and hadn't even been able to avoid summer math camp. Everything about Yanka flung a fat middle finger into the face of propriety. The more I learned, the more I wanted to know. I asked a friend in Siberia to order a book about her life for me, a 607-page collection of essays, photographs, and interviews. It took two months to arrive and two more to actually read, but by the time I was finished, I'd made up my mind: my next record would be an album covering the music of Yanka Dyagileva.

That's how the Punk Monk found me, through the blog of a Russian rock critic who posted a couple of demos of the Yanka covers I'd recorded in my bedroom. He wrote to tell me that he liked my versions. He was a huge Yanka fan too and had even contributed an article to the Yanka anthology I had read. Are you really a monk? I'd asked. Yes, came the reply, and a priest as well. Are there more of you? No, he admitted, we punk monks are still pretty rare birds.

I asked the Punk Monk for help decoding Yanka's lyrics for the liner notes of my album and we struck up a regular correspondence. At first, I tried to ignore the fact that he was a monk

SEPTEMBER 4, 1966

YANA STANISLAVOVNA DYAGILEVA WAS BORN IN THE SIBERIAN CITY OF NOVOSIBIRSK.

EVEN BY SOVIET STANDARDS, HER FAMILY WAS NOT WELL OFF. THEIR SMALL WOODEN HOUSE HAD NO INDOOR PLUMBING.

GROWING UP, YANKA KEPT TO HERSELF AND FILLED NOTEBOOKS WITH POETRY. UNLIKE MOST RUSSIAN GIRLS HER AGE, YANKA DRESSED SIMPLY AND MODESTLY. SHE DIDN'T WEAR MAKEUP AND PREFERRED BOOTS TO HIGH HEELS.

APRIL 1987

YANKA MET YEGOR LETOV, LEAD SINGER FOR THE LEGENDARY PUNK BAND CIVIL DEFENCE, AT THE FIRST NOVOSIBIRSK ROCK FESTIVAL.

SHE RETURNED WITH HIM TO HIS NATIVE CITY OF OMSK, BUT RIGHT AWAY THEY RAN INTO TROUBLE.

THE INTERNAL POLICE TRIED TO HAVE THE CONTROVERSIAL LETOV COMMITTED TO AN INSTITUTION. IT WAS A TACTIC SOVIET AUTHORITIES OFTEN USED TO BREAK THE WILL OF ARTISTS AND "DISSIDENTS." LETOV MANAGED TO ESCAPE, AND TOGETHER WITH YANKA, HE FLED SIBERIA.

ACCORDING TO LETOV, THEY "TRAVELED THE WHOLE COUNTRY, LIVED WITH HIPPIES, SANG SONGS ON THE STREET, ATE WHATEVER GOD PROVIDED, STOLE FOOD FROM THE MARKETS..."

THEY SURVIVED ON LESS THAN 40 CENTS A DAY, EATING IN MUNICIPAL CAFETERIAS AND SLEEPING IN BASEMENTS, ABANDONED TRAIN CARS, AND ATTICS.

IT WAS ON THE ROAD WITH LETOV THAT YANKA FIRST BEGAN PERFORMING AS A BACKUP SINGER FOR CIVIL DEFENCE.

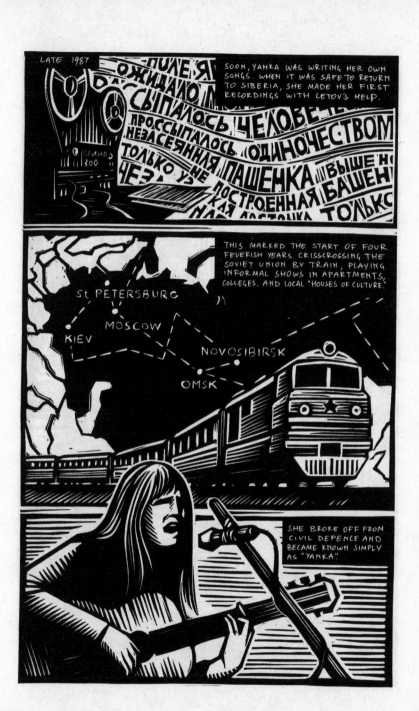

YANKA'S MUSIC WAS A HYBRID OF SIBERIAN PUNK, WESTERN ROCK, AND TRADITIONAL RUSSIAN FOLK. SHE USED TO TRAVEL TO SIBERIAN VILLAGES HERSELF TO MAKE FIELD RECORDINGS OF OLD SONGS.

HER SONGS WERE IRONIC TANGLES OF COMMUNIST SLOGANS, RUSSIAN FAIRY TALES, ARMY ANTHEMS.

THE APOCALYPTIC IMPRESSIONS OF A FADING NATION.

POSTCARDS FROM HER INNER STATE.

YANKA RECORDED WHEN SHE COULD, IN HOME STUDIOS AND ON CHEAP PORTABLE CASSETTE PLAYERS. THOSE RECORDINGS WERE NEVER RELEASED COMMERCIALLY DURING HER LIFETIME, BUT CIRCULATED HAND-TO-HAND AS SAMIZDAT.

SHE ACQUIRED A DEVOTED CULT FOLLOWING.

AS YANKA'S FAME GREW, THE SOVIET UNION UNRAVELED. SHE WAS SHOCKED BY SASHBASH'S SUICIDE IN 1988.

HER RELATIONSHIP WITH LETOV—NEVER EASY OR WELL DEFINED—FELL APART A YEAR LATER.

YANKA CONTINUED TO TOUR, BUT BATTLED DEPRESSION.

NOVOSIBIRSK, 1991

YANKA MOVED BACK TO THE WOODEN HOUSE OF HER CHILDHOOD. SHE MADE WHAT WOULD BE HER LAST RECORDINGS AND GREW INCREASINGLY ISOLATED.

MAY 9, 1991

AFTER GOING OUT FOR A WALK NEAR HER FATHER'S DACHA, YANKA DISAPPEARED. HER BODY WAS FOUND IN THE NEARBY INYA RIVER. SHE WAS 24 YEARS OLD.

LESS THAN SIX MONTHS LATER, THE U.S.S.R. COLLAPSED.

and stay focused on Russian idiomatic expressions and Soviet pop-cultural references, but soon found myself slipping into a confessional mode. One night after playing a bar in Omaha, Nebraska, I propped my laptop on a scabbed table and began tapping out questions for the Punk Monk. Am I doing the right thing? I wrote. Does this make any sense to you? I explained how "this" changed every day. Today "this" could be the fact that I'd gone to the trouble of getting a Canadian work permit only to arrive at a taqueria in Toronto and learn that five bands had been booked for the three available slots. Tomorrow "this" might be forgetting my wallet in a bakery in Eugene, Oregon, and realizing it six hours later when stopping for gas in a rural town near Mount Shasta.

"It makes perfect sense," the Punk Monk replied. "Any job contains such small and a bit foolish details. Even that of priest. In fact, if our job will contain only serious things we are interested in, it will be not useful to our souls. This is exactly what you are supposed to be doing. This is your path."

This didn't feel like a path, I thought to myself. Rather, it felt like the deliberate avoidance of some other definite and more sensible path that had suggested itself to me many times in the past. But this little bit of encouragement, which I found myself enjoying immensely, also had the unintended consequence of tapping into a wellspring of self-indulgence, my endless appetite for enumerating the problems I compulsively—almost cheerfully!— kept inserting into an otherwise problem-free life. "Everything feels very unstable," I began, "and I am considering just dropping all this and going back to living a life of quiet desperation . . ." Lately, the issue was that whenever I worked my day job, I felt paralyzed by guilt for neglecting music. Yet whenever I switched my attention to music, I found myself overcome by self-loathing, undone by the sheer impracticality of noodling entire days away on the guitar. The real problem here was that I lacked both the discipline to embrace the hedonistic lifestyle art-making required and the pragmatism to undertake one of those careers that deliver you to your future as predictably as a Japanese bullet train. Because these thoughts were so troubling, much of my time was spent ensuring I had no time to spend. The successful artists I knew always made the most of any spare hour. Given a day off, they might print up some stickers featuring their website and likeness, and spend the afternoon blithely affixing them to public property. For me, days off turned catastrophic. Oh, they might get off to a banging start, with the brave intention of writing a new song or two. But ten minutes into the project, I would notice that this new song sounded troublingly like my old songs. More intrusive thoughts would quickly squirm through this first chink in my self-confidence. *You do realize that no one is waiting for this new song? No one cares whether it is in the key of A or G, or how long the bridge is. No one cares whether you manage to rhyme* Tanqueray *with* Le Carré, *or, for that matter, whether this song ever gets written at all. But go on—write it! Stick it on top of the pile with all the other old-sounding new songs . . .* After these thoughts spent some time crashing about in my head, I'd decide it was time for a break. Better still, a bath! And while reflecting in the bath, it would occur to me that no matter how hard I work, I will never grow up to be an old black woman like the singers I most admire. My angst would thicken, first into a stew, then a gumbo, as the hours slipped by unnoticed, until suddenly it was time for dinner, then bed. Before I knew it, I was back at my day job, lamenting the time I didn't have to write new songs.

I wrote these thoughts out for the Punk Monk and then went to sleep on the floor of a man who may or may not have been the sound guy at the Replay Lounge in Lawrence, Kansas. I couldn't understand whether he was the real sound guy or just some guy replacing the sound guy who didn't show up. In any case, I did understand that he had a room to spare and that I could sleep there. But of course, it turned out to be very cold on the floor and I didn't sleep at all. Which meant I didn't wake up in the morning, I simply arose from the sleep I didn't have, from my seven-hour sprawl on the floor, feeling bludgeoned. And since there wasn't any coffee on hand to reach for, I reached for my computer instead and found I had a reply from the Punk Monk.

"When you are not working on yourself," the message read, "the world starts to work on you instead. People lose their identity and, then, integrity and start to live by two or more lives, none of them being worth to be lived. In this way, desperations are inevitable. You must acquire the skill to be yourself."

Perhaps it was the deadening sensation in my head, but considering the source, I was starting to have trouble with these Deepak Chopra–y pronouncements. For one thing, it seemed to me like the path of punk rock and the path of priesthood were two distinctly separate paths, running in opposite directions. And if the Punk Monk himself was a living oxymoron, just another weird, muddled mess, like all the other weird, muddled messes I typically surrounded myself with, what good, really, was all this advice about path-finding and self-being? Again, the following day, in Denver, I had my reply.

"Some time ago," the Punk Monk wrote, "I defined for myself a 'right' image of the Church as a church where Yanka could be a parishioner. There are all manner of churches in the world. The first thing is to establish your relationship with God, the next to find a church where you feel at home. Did you know that Yanka also converted before she died? She was baptized into the Russian Orthodox Church."

I hadn't known. But the next morning, as I drifted down I-70 west toward Salt Lake City, listening to Yanka, I found myself thinking about her conversion, wondering what it was that made her do it. It didn't matter, I told myself. It didn't save her. Religion was an insufficient guardrail. She ended up dead in the river, an apparent suicide, alone and rootless and looking for a comfort she'd never find. And yet . . . and yet, what to do with all this driving, driving, driving? Everything just going on and pointlessly on? The sky above northern Utah, too big. Idaho blurring by, a waste of gas. If I could convince myself that I was, indeed, on a path—a God-given path, not just some hideously circuitous highway mocking me with its metaphoric significance—*then* I could really get on with this hopeless to-ing and fro-ing. Once freed from logic, the singing to indifferent audiences, the failure to sleep on various floors, could all be undertaken with a renewed sense of purpose.

When I got home from touring, I was surprised to discover that I actually owned a Bible. Not some shoddy paperback cribbed from the nightstand of a Motel 6 either, but a handsome hardcover version that weighed as much as a full bottle of Jim Beam. How had I failed to notice it there on the shelf, right next to Jenna Jameson's autobiography, for what must have been years? I remember I once tried to read the Old Testament and made it as far as Judges. It got off to a rousing start, I recall, with the slaughter of ten thousand men. But by the time Jael bent down and drove a nail into Sisera's head, I was done. I knew I could never meet this God's stringent requirements; I didn't have the self-discipline. If He ever told me to follow Lot out of Brooklyn and never once look back, I would simply hand over my keys and my cell phone and prepare to become a condiment.

Now I decided I would give the New Testament a try; I had higher hopes for Jesus. But I quickly found that, like everyone, the Messiah had his good days and his bad days. He could be belligerent. He was maddeningly self-contradictory. Occasionally?

He smote things. But I was also surprised to find that Jesus some-times said things that I found comforting, that stayed with me.

"Do not be anxious about tomorrow, for tomorrow will be anxious for itself," said Jesus in Matthew 6. "Let the day's own trouble be sufficient for the day."

So true, I thought to myself. Don't be greedy. There will always be more trouble tomorrow. I jotted the verse down on a notecard and taped it up next to my desk. Soon there were a lot of notecards taped up around my desk.

"How can you say to your brother, 'Let me take the speck out of your eye,' when there is the log in your own eye?"

Right again. Don't be a hypocrite. With a two-by-four in your eye, you can't do much of anything, let alone deal with some-body else's speck.

"Salt is good; but if salt has lost its taste, how shall its salt-ness be restored?"

This last verse, from Luke 14, was a conundrum. But I liked that first declarative phrase, the rare glimpse into Jesus' season-ing preferences. Jesus thought that salt was good. And now I could picture Jesus salting things. Maybe regretting the extra shake, worrying about his sodium intake. He came into focus for me then. Myself, I'd take wild mushroom risotto over a Hostess cupcake any day. Jesus and I may not have a lot in common, I thought to myself, but we could come together on salt.

It was something.

Growing up with no religious affiliation, I always figured that I had only two options if I wanted to get with God: the Judaism of my father's side of the family or the Russian Orthodox Christi-anity of my mother's side. But since everyone on both sides of my family was raised atheist, they didn't leave me with much to go on. When I was five or six, I remember asking Mama what would happen to me after I died. We were eating lunch in a restaurant on Cape Cod with a group of my mother's friends. I knew it probably wasn't the best occasion to bring it up, but we'd driven past a graveyard earlier that afternoon and a panicked scribbling feeling had been rising in my chest ever since. I remember the conversation stopping after I asked my question, and Mama looking down at me from what seemed like a great height.

"They'll put you in a box in the ground and you will rot there," she said, raising the two black lines that had long since replaced her eyebrows. "And?"

Papa was Jewish, but only on paper. New Yorkers, thanks to alternate-side-parking suspension days, had a familiarity with holidays like Shavuot, Simchas Torah, and Shemini Atzereth that my father could only dream of. Nonetheless, this didn't stop him from coming up with his own ideas. When I was maybe seven or eight years old, I asked Papa whether he believed in God. My father, the theoretical physicist, thought this over for a long time; he took philosophical questions, even those from young children, very seriously. (Later, when I was in college, he received a letter from a nine-year-old girl claiming to have discovered the secrets of the universe while watching the toilet bowl drain—she received a long and thoughtful handwritten reply.)

Finally, Papa said, "Well, it depends. Do you mean the kind of god people worship on Earth? Like Jesus, Allah, Vishnu? That kind of god?"

Even as a small child, I knew that something had gone terribly wrong. What other kind of god was there apart from the ones we knew on Earth? I confirmed for Papa, with some hesitation, that yes, I was only concerned with Earth. The planet we lived on.

"Ah, then I guess to answer your question I would have to say no, I don't believe in that kind of god."

It was obvious that Papa was holding out on me, so I went ahead and asked the question he'd been waiting for.

"So what kind of god *do* you believe in?"

"You see," Papa began, "Earth is just one of an infinite number of planets in an ever-expanding universe. Chances are that ours isn't the best planet. It's probably, you know, just a really average planet. Average people, average ideas, average gods," and here Papa paused, lighting up a little. "But of course that means that there are other planets out there that have the best of everything, and maybe one of these planets is inhabited by a being wiser and more enlightened than anyone we can imagine. Maybe this being is already guiding our actions here on Earth. Things that we think we are doing and deciding for ourselves might in fact be the invisible work of this ultimate being." Papa's eyes were far away. He seemed to have drifted off to a soft and happy place.

I blinked at him. *This* is what Papa believed?

"Are you talking about, like, a space alien from . . . outer space?" I asked.

"Yes, that's exactly what I'm talking about!" Papa said excitedly.

I thanked him and went away.

In Massachusetts the winters are long and fierce and the houses, both new and old, are stubbornly drafty. Since they don't hold heat, and heating them is expensive, people have gotten used to walking around wearing three turtlenecks and pretending this is normal. Mine was the only bedroom on the bottom floor of my family's two-story house. It lay within a special microclimate whose damp, pervasive chill called to mind certain parts of northern Canada. The night that Papa offered me his God-as-space-alien theory, I remember lying in my narrow bed, watching my breath billow whitely in the air above me, trying to envision the being Papa had described. In my head, the space-alien God looked something like a giant praying mantis. He had massive green eyes the size of satellite dishes that trembled with a luminous, otherworldly understanding, and he was dressed a bit like Papa, who favored slacks from Banana Republic, long-sleeved linen shirts, and the occasional vest or blazer with suede elbow patches. He never said anything but only stared at me un-blinkingly, his antennae quivering with wisdom and empathy. Over many months, I did my best to believe in the praying man-tis, but in the end, his presence on the very best of planets in a faraway universe just didn't offer much in the way of guidance or comfort to my earthbound self. That was when I realized that I would just have to settle for a mediocre god, somewhere closer to home.

Babushka was the only member of the family who had been baptized Russian Orthodox, and this was something I was al-ways interested in discussing with her. The only problem was that Babushka pretended to be Jewish. She did this because abso-lutely every one of her friends—practically every Russian émigré of that era—was Jewish, and it was uncomfortable for her to go against the grain. She had married a Jew and this provided her with enough cover to pass. She kept a photograph of her grand-parents' traditional Orthodox wedding hidden deep in her un-derwear drawer and lived instead among the props: the menorah, the Hebrew calendar, some boxes of matzoh meal artfully scat-tered around the kitchen.

A couple of years ago at my mother's annual Christmas party, Babushka put down her fork to make a sudden and por-tentous announcement.

"I am a conformist," she said, looking around the table slowly and deliberately, making sure to give each of us the eye. "I am normal. What all people do, I do too."

It was as though Babushka had just announced that she was gay. Her look said: This is something about me that is unchanging, something I am proud of, and you just have to accept if you really love me. But the truth was that, at eighty-nine years old, we were all just happy to have her wake up in the morning, slip on a leopard-print dress, and enjoy a few good reruns of *Knots Landing*. If Babushka had instead told us she'd decided to wear only a tutu and eat nothing but whipped cream for breakfast, lunch, and dinner, I would have been on my way to Costco faster than you could say "Cool Whip." As it was, we all reassured her that a conformist was a very fine thing to be and that she should go right ahead being one. Needless to say, this episode went a long way toward explaining how she felt about religion.

So I was on my own. Clearly the easiest choice, in the liberal suburb where I grew up, would have been just to become Jewish. It felt like a particularly civilized hobby I could mellow into, like joining a curling league. Maybe this was because the rabbi at the reformed synagogue in town, the one all of my Jewish friends attended, was an avowed atheist. This didn't seem to stir up much controversy; on the contrary, there was an almost palpable sense of relief that without the messy and emotional business of God muddying the waters, the rabbi could finally focus on the more important issue of what it really meant to be a Jew. Jewish friends never mentioned God either, though they maintained an obsessive interest in their Jewish youth group and the overnight trips affording tantalizing make-out opportunities with the exotic Jews of neighboring Winchester. Only once did Papa make a visit to this synagogue, to recite the Mourner's Kaddish when his father died. He described the experience like this:

"First there was a guy who played guitar. Then another guy came out and warned us not to support President Bush. Then finally this sort of fat, spiritual guy came out and read the Kaddish. That last part was okay. I guess."

Josh had attended Hebrew School for eight years at this temple, and the only trace left of the whole experience was the perverse delight he took in playing a celebrity guessing game called Jew or Not Jew. (Jon Stewart? Jew! Conan O'Brien? Not Jew.)

Now I know that there are Jewish people somewhere in Crown Heights who would have been happy to introduce me to the rigors and joys of living life according to the Halakha, but these were not the people I knew. Based on my very limited perspective, becoming a Jew meant joining an organization that combined elements of Mensa, JDate, and the world's most selective book club. But I guess the good thing about growing up without religion is that you can really dream big. I was never subjected to early morning sermons on things I didn't care about. I was never forced to repeat the inane stuff my parents believed until I snapped one day and we ended up circling a deflated kiddie pool on the front lawn, screaming obscenities at one another while reality television cameras rolled. I didn't grow up with a desperate fear of my own bodily functions, nor were there videos of me singing embarrassing songs about angels anywhere on YouTube.

So I figured there was no need for bottom-feeding now. Sure, embracing any religion involves compromise and the inevitable adjustment of expectations. But if choosing a religion was like finding a mate, I didn't want to settle for the spiritual equivalent of a tubby guy named Earl, whose psoriasis of the scalp would keep me busy dusting seatbacks for the next forty years. I could afford to set the bar high, so I did. For example: no houses of worship in strip malls. How could I commune with the Holy Spirit with my thighs stuck to a metal folding chair and the smell of fried chicken still emanating from the stained acoustic tiles overhead? Similarly, I found prayer unlikely in one of those spiritual centers designed to make office workers comfortable, a place with headachy fluorescent lights, Muzak piped into the bathrooms, and an ATM in the lobby. I wanted to worship in a church that looked like it had been plucked out of a Hans Christian Andersen story, and didn't think that was too much to ask. Unfortunately, the reformed synagogue in my town also didn't meet this criterion; it was designed by a fancy architect, with a swooping roof and the kind of airy lobby reminiscent of Ivy League universities or cancer research institutes. This seemed like a good place to debate education reform with reasonable, well-meaning people, but to commune with God? Honestly, where was the mystery? The spontaneous healing? The speaking in tongues? The casting off of demons? Why endure the tedium and strictures of religion without any of the fun stuff? No, I decided, not for me. I was going to hold out. I knew exactly what I wanted. I wanted unreasonable people believing impossible things. I wanted unicorns.

Maybe this was because my family, like the white queen in Alice in Wonderland, had a penchant for believing impossible things. The notion that "certain people have powers" was something calmly and unquestioningly accepted by everyone but me. My grandmother still regretted a particular encounter my grandfather had with a Gypsy who laid a curse on them in 1957. They had just stepped off a train to stretch their legs, somewhere between Babushka's native St. Petersburg, where they had been visiting relatives, and their home in Kharkov, when the Gypsy approached my grandfather.

"Dorogoy, dorogoy!" Dear one, dear one, she called out. "Silver my palm and I will read your fortune."

"Thanks, but I don't need a fortune," my grandfather said. "I don't believe in them." My grandfather was that kind of clear-eyed thinker before he came to the States and discovered scratch lotto.

"Believe or don't believe," she intoned darkly, "have it your way, but two blows await you when you return home." And with that the Gypsy turned and swept off down the platform.

"Don't worry," my grandfather assured Babushka. "She's just trying to spoil our good mood."

But when they arrived back in Kharkov they found, in a Kafkaesque twist, that their apartment had been occupied by another couple. They waited out the night in the cramped living room of a friend, and the next morning the second blow was dealt: their best friends, a couple they loved like family, were giving up on the Soviet Union and returning home to Romania.

"See?" Babushka would say. "She didn't say ten blows, did she? No! She said two blows. And that's exactly what we got—one on the first day and the second on the next. It is proof there really are people who can see into the future. That Gypsy—she was like Nostradamus or our famous psychic Juna, who treated Brezhnev himself!"

I recall a similar discussion with my parents over a paper on the Russian Revolution I was writing for my high school European history class. My father and I were sitting in our usual positions at the kitchen table while the news blared on the television. Mama was at the counter making a salad. I had just returned from the Copley library and had some exciting news to report regarding Tsar Nicholas II.

"I can't believe Tsar Nicholas refused the Duma's request to grant a constitution!"

My parents nodded sympathetically. This was something they'd evidently heard about before.

"He fired Grand Duke Nicholas and then totally mismanaged the war!"

My parents agreed: it was true, the last tsar had run the country into the ground.

"And what about Rasputin? The Romanovs, like, believed everything he said. They actually thought that guy had magic powers!"

At this Mama stopped, her knife frozen over the glistening half dome of a tomato. My father turned his eyes away from Peter Jennings, whose voice seemed to recede to a murmur.

"Well," Papa began, a bit reproachfully, "Rasputin *did* have powers. That much we know is true."

"Absolutely!" Mama seconded. "He used his powers to cure the tsarevich's hemophilia." And with that, the realist who assured me that nothing more than a rotting grave awaits us in death calmly went back to quartering her tomato.

"Seriously, guys—" I began, nervously. But Papa, sensing where I was heading, cut me off.

"Look, some people are really good at math, right? And some people are great violin players, right? Well, then there are people with different talents. Like they are good at healing people with their hands. Understand?"

Then Papa turned back to Peter Jennings in a way that invited no further discussion, and I was left holding the bag again, the irrational pragmatist stubbornly denying things that were obviously true.

The same magical thinking extended to the realm of health. My mother rejected the idea of doctors. She didn't believe in them. Fevers raged, heavy things fell on her, whatever—Mama kept plowing forward in her crusade against the dubious accuracy of double-blind, randomized, controlled trials with the dedication of a hard-core Christian Scientist. Meanwhile, Papa, the world-renowned physicist, preferred alternative medicine— although I daresay that the "healers" he visited might, with the help of an *Oxford English Dictionary*, be more accurately defined as "witches" or "warlocks." They ranged from acupuncturists and homeopaths, at the respectable end of things, to people he absolutely refused to discuss with me no matter how much I pleaded or promised not to make fun of him. And then there was

Babushka, with her weird Russian folk remedies and assortment of scarily pungent tinctures lining the shelves of the linen closet. Not long ago she called me, complaining of an infected cut, and when I suggested, with the dumbness of a rubber mallet, that she go see a doctor, she replied, "Don't worry, Lastochka, I taped half an onion to my arm and it feels much better now."

I still remember my first visit to a Russian Orthodox church. It took place during a trip to Chita, a breathtakingly cold, rugged, and isolated swath of eastern Siberia bordering China and Mongolia to the south and permafrost and more ice to the north. In my mid-twenties, I took a job with an obscure nonprofit organization that recruited volunteer English teachers and sent them to work in high schools and universities in the distant Russian province. The organization was not without a sense of humor regarding its mission and even sold stickers that read, "Do you know where Chita is? I do!" When I got the job, I gave one to Papa, and he gleefully stuck it to the back of his Honda, where it stayed for years until Mama finally made him steam it off.

An English teacher at the state university offered to take me to Sunday services. The prospect of waking up in the cold blue morning and trudging over streets of broken asphalt where the manhole covers often liked to go missing did not elicit the same enthusiasm as, say, the offer of a spiked hot cider would have, but it was clearly the polite thing to do. I remember that when we reached the church, a modest wooden building painted a cheery light blue, I did what everyone else did, stopping at the threshold to cross myself vigorously with the wrong hand. Inside, the air was thick with the smell of burning beeswax and incense.

I was surprised to find the church packed and the crowd a decidedly unfrumpy one. There were men in muscle shirts wearing oversized gold crosses on chains thick as lasso rope, and women who had dressed with all the concern for warmth or modesty of a person making a journey from the shower to the bedroom. Stepping forward to shield my gaze from the exposed midriff of the woman in front of me, my guide felt compelled to apologize.

"Some of these people care nothing about God, of course, for them this is all just a"—she motioned at the crowd—"a fashion statement."

I looked around again and saw that, among the crowd, there were also those easily identified as "true believers," mostly elderly men and stocky women with their heads covered and a small cache of sober young people who were similarly unadorned. All in all, I felt comfortable enough; the congregation really looked no different from the passengers on a typical Q express train.

Russian Orthodox services often last more than three hours, during which you have to stand. There are no pews. The service is also conducted entirely in Church Slavonic, a language that fell out of literary use in Russia more than two hundred years ago. I couldn't understand anything, and because I am barely five feet tall, I could hardly see anything either. In the distance, there seemed to be a man with a long beard wearing a boxy golden dress, waving a candle sword—three long tapers stuck into an ornate hilt. Yet I could still hear the choir. I could smell the incense and feast my eyes on icons that seemed to glisten and weep in the candlelight. Quite simply: it was beautiful. But after only half an hour my guide was tugging at my coat. Apparently she had a busy day of sightseeing planned for us. We were already behind schedule, and I didn't want to miss out on a visit to the Memorial of War and Labor Glory of the Transbaikaliana during the Great Patriotic War, did I?

When I returned home from Russia, I told Papa about my visit to the church, how I'd enjoyed it.

"I'm going to tell you a little story that I never shared with you before," Papa said, taking an orange from the bowl on the kitchen table. "Do you remember when you were in third grade and we sent you to that Christian summer camp?"

I did. The camp was called Meadow Breeze and it was run by an evangelical Christian school not far from where we lived.

"You used to come home from camp and beg me and Mama to just let Jesus into our hearts. You'd get so worked up about it." He stopped, chuckling at the memory. "We used to laugh at you."

"Right," I said, not a little impatiently. "So?"

"Well, not long after you finished camp, I went to Italy for a physics conference and I happened to get very sick. Something like the flu. And I had a fever that kept getting worse. I remember thinking to myself: A person could easily die this way, *I could die this very night*, far away from my family in a foreign country with no one to turn to for help . . . I don't know, maybe I was just delirious."

"Wow. So, what did you do?"

"Well, I remembered what you said."

"What did I say?"

"You said to let Jesus into my heart." Papa looked down, peeling his orange. "So I decided to try it. I said to myself, 'Okay, Jesus, please heal me. I am totally and sincerely opening my heart to you.' Then I kind of spread my arms open just like this on the bedspread." Papa held his arms out like he was getting a pat-down at the airport.

"Holy shit, so then what happened?" I dropped a piece of orange on the floor, managing to wipe it against my jeans before sticking it in my mouth.

"I was healed."

"What?"

"I was healed. Within an hour my fever was gone. That was it."

The kitchen was quiet. Papa set the orange on the table, then popped the peel into his mouth. I didn't really know what to say. What was he trying to tell me? That he was a believer now? That I had the right idea back when I was a brainwashed child with a heart full of Jesus? It was the first time we'd talked about religion since that long-ago discussion about alien theology. Recently, a statue of Buddha had appeared on Papa's desk. I took that as a hopeful sign that he was coming to terms with life on a mediocre planet and our limited menu of gods. But when it came to what my father thought, I conceded that I could easily be wrong about everything. For all I knew, he was building a spaceship in the garage.

"I don't even know why I'm telling you this," Papa said, chewing his orange peel.

Because I couldn't just drive around the country singing and losing money every day, I also worked a part-time job at a small consulting company with clients in Russia. One day, after I'd been corresponding with the Punk Monk for about six months, my boss asked if I would be willing to spend a month in Siberia to help evaluate a project. I wrote to the Punk Monk right away. I had family in St. Petersburg and figured I could stop by for a visit on the way home. But the Punk Monk surprised me by suggesting we meet in Novosibirsk instead, the city where Yanka was born, and where she was also buried.

"We can visit Yanka's grave together and I will perform the Panikhída," the Punk Monk wrote.

"What's that?" I asked.

"Orthodox funerary rite."

The Punk Monk flew out to Novosibirsk every year to perform the rites at Yanka's grave on May 9, the anniversary of her death. This year he would make an extra trip. We set a date: October 13, my birthday.

The night before our visit to the cemetery, I waited for the Punk Monk at my hotel, the Golden Valley in Akademgorodok. He'd asked me to meet him here, at the bar on the eighth floor, and so I sat at a plain wooden table, nervously waiting, chewing on some stale pistachios. Two guys at a neighboring table called over, offering to buy me a drink. I shook my head.

"It doesn't matter." One of the men laughed, watching me switch my wedding ring to my right hand, as is customary in Russia. "Your husband's not here anyway." He had a rough face and a neck that flowed over his shirt collar, pale and white as champagne foam.

"Yes, he is," I shot back. "In fact, he's on his way." Now I'd done it, ensnared myself in a web of sacrilegious lies. The pistachios were too salty. I thought of Jesus and felt slightly ill.

When the Punk Monk arrived a moment later, I noticed he looked like neither a punk nor a monk. He looked a bit like a dad. A dad who seemed to be engaged in some sort of exotic beard-off, but nonetheless. The Punk Monk greeted me warmly. I wanted to give him a hug, but didn't dare, even though he was supposed to be my husband. I didn't know what to do with myself. The waitress came by, and the Punk Monk ordered a beer.

"Are you allowed to drink beer?" I asked. I had assumed monks weren't allowed to do anything.

"Beer, yes. But not vodka. I like it too much," the Punk Monk said. "It almost killed me once."

As I struggled to absorb this new piece of information I ordered a beer for myself as well, even though I disliked beer and, in fact, disliked Russian beer even more than the American beer I already made a point of not drinking. The waitress left and I opened my mouth to ask the Punk Monk to tell me about the time vodka almost killed him.

"So where do you live?" I asked instead.

"I live with my mother."

"Oh," I said. "Isn't that a little . . . inconvenient?"

"Not really," the Punk Monk replied, serenely. "Why would it be?"

"I don't know." I said, taking a sip of hateful beer. Only, of course, I did know.

Then the Punk Monk drained his glass and announced he was heading to bed. The flight from St. Petersburg had been tiring.

I stood up as well, wondering whether the men at the neighboring table were still watching, and if I should find some pretext to follow the Punk Monk to his room—*our* room—but when I turned around, the men were already gone.

Arriving downstairs in the morning, I found the Punk Monk already waiting for me by the front door. There was snow on the ground, the air raw and stinging. I was wearing long underwear. A heavy sweater under my full-length coat. Hat and gloves. The Punk Monk let his jacket flap open, indifferent to the cold. We traveled by bus and by car, for nearly an hour, past the artificial sea and the belching factories and the husks of unfinished buildings. Blocks of concrete bled into the colorless sky, one pale wash. Eventually, the buildings gave way to fir trees, the snow grew cleaner. When we arrived at the gates of the Zaeltsovsky Cemetery, the Punk Monk asked me to wait outside the tiny chapel. A moment later, he emerged with a little paper bag.

"A present," he said. "For you." He held the bag out to me.

Inside was a wooden Russian Orthodox cross and a Bible. I opened the Bible. It was written in Church Slavonic.

"I can't read this."

"True," the Punk Monk said.

Then he walked through the cemetery gates and I followed. The central lane was lined with the graves of gangsters. Lifelike portraits of paunchy men in tracksuits, holding bottles of Georgian wine or dangling the keys to a Mercedes, grinned down at us from towering slabs of granite. They did not look like drug dealers and murderers; they looked like people enjoying a barbecue on the Jersey Shore. We walked along, giggling and pointing, until the paths grew narrower. Then the asphalt ended and there was nothing to do but follow the handmade signs left by fans, a telltale ribbon, an arrow carved into a tree trunk. The Punk Monk left the path and cut through the graves, his feet crunching over the snow-covered mounds. I jogged to keep up. This part of the cemetery had long been left untended; the ground was bumpy and uneven, trees grew at odd angles. Then, suddenly, the Punk Monk stopped. There it was—a little fenced-in plot with Yanka's grave, her stepbrother's alongside it. The marker was plain. A gray slab with her black-and-white photograph inside a white oval. Some dead flowers. A few weeks ago, back in the States, I'd thought about this moment and cried. Standing here now, I only felt cold.

The Punk Monk sat himself at a nearby bench. He removed a long black robe from his bag and slipped it over his head. Then he pulled out a giant chain with a heavy Orthodox cross and draped it around his neck. He set some black pucks of charcoal on the bench in front of him.

"I just need to light the censer and we can get started."

The Punk Monk reached into his backpack to pull out the censer. He fumbled around inside the bag for a moment, then held up his hand, indicating: wait.

"Damn," he said, holding the censer up for me to see. "The chains are tangled."

The censer looked as though the Punk Monk had dropped it into a blender, punched the "ice crush" button, and gone to brush his teeth.

We bent our heads together and went to work. Twenty minutes later, when my fingers were blue and numb, I dropped my end of the chain and stood up to stretch. I walked over to Yanka's grave, rubbing my hands together, trying to warm them. From there I saw the Punk Monk bent over the censer, his face a mask of concentration as he struggled with the knots. After a moment, he sensed me staring and looked up.

"I'm sorry about this." The Punk Monk gestured at the hopeless mess of chain. Then he laughed, loudly and happily, as though we weren't surrounded by acres of dead people, freezing our asses off in the middle of a Siberian forest.

"I wish I could say it's the first time this has ever happened to me."

"Punk Monk?"

"Yes?"

The words were out of my mouth before I could stop them. "Would you baptize me?"

The Punk Monk eyed me suspiciously before he spoke.

"I don't do sprinkling," he said. "Only full immersion."

"Okay," I said, and rejoined him at the bench, where I took up my end of the censer once more. Then without another word, we bent our heads and got back to work.

I decided not to tell anyone. The signposts that marked the way to my conversion—Yanka, the acoustics underwater, the goodness of salt, a disorganized priest—all aligned perfectly in my head, but I knew other people would find ways to poke holes in my airtight logic. In particular, I feared Josh would unravel me with a few pointed questions. And I worried the dormant Jew in him might get upset. Would he still want to play Jew or Not Jew together? Better to convert now and ask questions later. I already had enough trouble for today.

The church turned out to be an easy place to hide. It still has no official address. To get there by cab, the Punk Monk had to give the driver directions to the medical center across the street. Redbricked and onion-domed, it sat tucked behind a nondescript kiosk selling flowers. Inside, the walls were each painted a different fruit-colored hue. They had been painted by hand, the Punk Monk told me, by parishioners. The icons covering the walls were also a potluck of styles—some Greek, some English, some Russian—most of them donated. The floor was covered with a buckling sheet of vinyl made to look like wooden parquet. It was a homemade kind of place. Another DIY venue, not so different from the converted churches I often played on tour.

The Punk Monk slipped through a side door near the altar and emerged in his vestments a few minutes later with a careworn Bible in his hand. He led me to a makeshift altar and proceeded to read the Nicene Creed in Old Church Slavonic, slowly and sonorously. I repeated the words after him, slowly and badly. He asked me to renounce Satan, then to spit on him three times. I renounced Satan, then spat on the nondescript patch of vinyl flooring the Punk Monk indicated. With Satan well spat on, I was led to a stainless steel vat sitting in the middle of the room. It looked like the kind of tank used to cure pickles. The Punk Monk blessed the water, swinging the censer freely over its surface, and then he pulled a chair up to the vat, and I understood it was time for me to climb inside. I lowered myself over the edge and felt the warm pressure of the water rise to my shoulders, the suddenly heavy cotton of my shapeless dress brushing against my skin. The Punk Monk placed his hand on top of my head. I took a deep breath and thought to myself: I am a conformist.

Then I stopped thinking, and went down.

THE BENEFITS OF SELF-CASTRATION

blamed my obsession with the castrati on Italy. I would even go so far as to claim it was a form of self-defense, because Italy keeps trying to kill me. Everyone tells me that I am supposed to love Italy. I do not. Partly this has to do with being a vegetarian—a culinary handicap in a country where the recipe for salting ham in a certain way is guarded with more care than a reporter visiting Pyongyang. And while I think pasta is okay, I am not about to adopt it as a personal religion. So my anxieties in Italy generally begin with my first meal as I wonder whether death by cheese overdose is a realistic possibility. More blasphemous thoughts are quick to follow. Italy is beautiful, I would say to myself, but why am I so bored here? Why is everyone always discussing tonight's dinner while today's lunch is still languishing in our mouths? Why does a debate about the relative sponginess of *bufala* inevitably escalate into violence? Why are there so many lonely, morose men lolling about reading Rilke and living with their mothers well into middle age? And where do they have sex? I did my best to tease out a response to this last question, but the answer always slipped away, elided by that legendary Italian charm. Eventually, one of the guys I toured with let drop that the grounds of the picturesque castle in his village served an important secondary function the tour guides failed to mention. This new information was helpful, but seemed to relegate sex to warm, dry weather.

The first time I toured Italy it was with four men stuffed into a Monterosso. In addition to the Italian trio I shared a bill with each night, there was our tour manager, Laurent, a Frenchman who happened to drive with the utmost of care. Unfortunately, Laurent had to return to his job in Toulouse a couple of days before the tour ended, which meant leaving me in the care of the Italians for our remaining shows. This news was worrisome because the Italians, though exceedingly charismatic and lovable, did not inspire confidence behind the wheel. For one thing, they were very prone to distraction on Italy's already dodgy highways. Within the space of ten seconds, they could go from speaking quietly in their beautiful, mellifluous tongue, to communicating in a violent form of hands-off-the-wheel sign language where the only words were go, *fuck*, and *yourself*. Moreover, getting to our remaining shows meant getting an early start, and mornings were a notoriously difficult time for the Italians, who required large quantities of cigarettes and five tiny espressos just to get over the tragedy of not being asleep anymore.

Laurent took me aside again one last time before leaving.

"Are you abzolutely zure eet vil be okay?" he asked, with a meaningful stare.

"Of course," I replied, full of false American bluster. "Don't worry, Laurent. Eat some more cheese! Be happy!"

Less than four hours later, we hit the truck.

To be fair to the Italians, it was not a serious accident. It might even have qualified as the world's slowest collision. The truck—a giant semi—was merging into our lane from the left, seemingly forever. I remember watching it ride alongside us, almost parallel with our tinfoil station wagon, until eventually we simply glided into each other and congealed, like two balls of polenta. There was the sound of tearing metal and then a shocked silence followed by the now familiar sound of Italians yelling at one another. My window disintegrated into a web of tiny crystals. They hung there for a moment and then began to fall softly into my hair, my lap, one by one. I got out of the car and stood on the side of the road calmly picking bits of glass out of my handbag while the Italians argued about whose fault it was. It was raining. Waiting there for the *militsia*, someone raised the question of whether it would be safe to continue on to our show that night despite the mangled bumper, lack of a driver's-side mirror, and a missing back window. The answer turned out to be yes.

Despite my misgivings, I was convinced to return to Italy a year later when an acquaintance of mine, a singer-songwriter from Canada, suggested we tour Europe together. He promised this time it would be fun. He knew people—artists and dancers and fire-eating clowns. There would be visits to ancient ruins and exotic Jewish graveyards. Stupidly, I agreed—because what lures me into vans and onto airplanes is never the promise of money, but rather the promise of fire-eating clowns and Jewish graveyards. Tickets were purchased, cars were rented, and a tour that spanned from the edge of Sicily to the northern border with Switzerland was booked.

Why was I unsurprised when everything fell apart two weeks before we were supposed to leave for Reggio Calabria? My Canadian friend canceled due to a family emergency, and all hope for fun and adventure suddenly became vanishingly small. Now my fate depended entirely on the opening act, an Italian man we will call Giuseppe, whom I'd never met. The new plan was to use

Giuseppe's car for the tour. As luck would have it, though, there was another last-minute *problemo*. Giuseppe knew nothing about what had happened during my last visit to Italy, but it turned out he'd also just gotten into a terrible car accident, one he swore was not his fault. His car was totaled, but not to worry, he re-assured me, we would do the tour in the replacement rental his insurance company had provided. I was not reassured.

During my first trip to Italy, I'd spent the entire tour en-grossed in a 576-page biography of Rasputin, the famous Rus-sian mystic whom my parents—both trained scientists—insisted possessed magical healing powers. When I was the only person in the Monterosso to remain stubbornly healthy despite the miser-able flulike ailment that reduced all of my tourmates to sweaty wraiths horking into their Proseccos, I had to concede that per-haps my parents were on to something. Now, in those last anx-ious days before I left for Italy to commence a tour with another car-crashing Italian, I needed a new book to bring along with me. A page-turner that would guarantee me nothing short of obliv-ion, a total eclipse of the outside world and everyone around me. That was when I realized that only *Castration and the Heavenly Kingdom* could save me.

I had Rasputin to thank for introducing me to the Skoptsy; he was rumored to be a member of a related sect, the Khlysty. The biography mentioned the Skoptsy only in passing, but one could not help being struck by the central tenet of their theology: the practice of self-castration as a means of excising sin. It was the kind of detail that really begs for more attention. So when I got back to the States, I decided to do some research. The Skoptsy, first documented in the eighteenth century, were led by a series of homegrown mystics who wandered from village to village, cas-trating the faithful. The tsarist regime condemned and scattered them, from the Romanian city of Yassi to the farthest reaches of Siberia, yet the Skoptsy continued to thrive throughout the nineteenth century. Membership in the sect was eventually rumored to reach the hundreds of thousands. What photographs I could find online showed somber people with fleshy cheeks and pasty skin, oozing moral rectitude and clutching white handkerchiefs in their laps as symbols of purity.

Without denying that there was something more than a little icky about castration, I couldn't help but admire the strength of their convictions. Among my dissolute circle of friends, everything was negotiable. If I said to one of them: "Consider this: Perhaps God is actually a pepperoni pizza?" they would scoff at me, yes, but not without that flash of self-doubt. I would see the questions hovering in their eyes: "Am I being too quick to judge? Could it all be a matter of semantics? What did she mean by that? I don't want to be a jerk. Maybe God *is* a pepperoni pizza?" For the Skoptsy, it was clearly all or nothing—God could never, under any circumstances, be a pepperoni pizza. And there was one other undeniable reason to admire them: cutting off your balls took balls.

I was shocked to find that *Castration and the Heavenly Kingdom* was the only book available in English about the Skoptsy. Greedily, I purchased it right away and gave it a prominent place on my bookshelf, where it surprised and mortified houseguests for the better part of a year. Although I sometimes weakened and let myself flip through the insert in the middle featuring grisly black-and-white photos of naked castrati, mostly I waited for a sign that the right moment to read it had finally arrived. Giuseppe's car crash, I decided, was that sign.

Giuseppe picked me up at the airport in Milan. On the way back to his apartment, he switched into reverse on a busy highway, traveled backward in the right lane for a good five hundred feet, then backed the wrong way down an off-ramp into a gas station he'd passed by accident. Normally, I would have found this kind of stunt to be quite alarming, but on that day it didn't matter—I was already well into the story of Kondratii Selivanov, the wandering serf and early Skopets leader who rose to prominence in St. Petersburg high society. A few nights later, when Giuseppe slid into the car still clutching a tumbler full of Negroni from the bar where we'd just played, and drove home while drinking, barely palming the wheel with his free hand, I was too concerned with how the Skoptsy would weather their exile to Yakutsk—the coldest inhabited region on earth—to pay much attention. But it wasn't until the last night of our tour that I realized the truly awesome power of the castrati to insulate and protect me.

It was our second-to-last show, and when the man approached me, I was sitting in a cavernous, cafeteria-like space in the community center in Trento, having just finished my sound check. As usual, I was reading *Castration and the Heavenly Kingdom*, and had become totally consumed by the tribulations of Nikifor Petrovich Latyshev, a long-suffering Skopets who lived well into the Stalin era.

"May I?" the man asked, gliding up and gesturing to the seat next to me. Reluctantly I nodded and put the book down. We were alone in a sea of empty tables and chairs.

"You will pardon me," he began with a conspiratorial smile, leaning forward, "but I wanted to tell you that I only came here tonight for you. To hear you sing."

"Is that right?" I asked brightly. I was deeply worried about Nikifor. It was 1932, his property had just been seized by the Soviet police, and they'd brought him in for questioning. What would they do once they learned he was a Skopets? Would Nikifor end up as just another victim thrown on the scrap heap of Stalin's brutal collectivization policies?

"Yes. My friend told me to come. He found you on the internet."

I couldn't disagree that the internet had a wonderful way of bringing people together.

"Can I buy you a beer?" the man asked, after a longish pause.

I didn't want a beer; I wanted to know whether Nikifor would be able to reclaim the little house he'd bought from Maria Bochkareva. Just four years earlier he'd been living peacefully with an elderly Skoptsina on a farmstead on the Kama River, raising cows and growing vegetables, but look at him now, with scarcely a potato to call his own . . .

"I actually get all the free beer I want for playing here tonight. But thank you."

The man cast a glance around the room, looking a bit desperate. "Perhaps something to eat then . . . ?" he said.

"The venue already gave me dinner—another little perk of being a performer, I guess." Here I tried to look wistful. "But it's really very nice of you to offer."

That is when his eyes lit hopefully upon the back cover of my book.

"Tell me," he said, "what's that you're reading?"

Without thinking, I flipped the book over and handed it to the man, who seemed to wither visibly as he considered its title.

"It's about the Skoptsy," I offered. "They were a self-castrating Christian sect from Russia."

"Sounds . . . painful," he said, struggling to recast his grimace into a smile.

"Well, the Skoptsy actually practiced *two* forms of castration, one they referred to as the minor seal and the other as the major seal. I'm sure each was bad enough on its own, but I bet going in for *both* would have qualified as a real home run painwise, don't you?"

The man was gone. He had slipped away, mumbling some excuse and leaving his glass of beer still half full on the table beside me. Without hesitating for a moment, I snatched up the book again, relieved to be reunited with Nikifor and very much hoping for some news about his elderly brother Fedor as well— but then I stopped, suddenly struck by the momentousness of what had just happened. Was it possible that I had just discovered the world's first light, portable, and nonadhesive Annoying Man Repellent? One that could reach its full potency only here, in Italy, where men worship nothing so much as their own balls? The Italians were like free-jazz players when it came to describing their balls, with each new variation corresponding to a specific note on the scale of human discomfort. I'd heard them all: Ey! Quit breaking my balls! Stop squeezing my balls! Resist poking my balls! Do not apply a vibrating cell phone to my balls! I didn't even know what Italian men would have left to say to one another if you took away their balls—they saw the world through ball-colored glasses. I gazed at the book, stunned, thinking this must be how those giant-squid hunters from Japan felt the first time the elusive *Architeuthis* swam into view. Did the author realize she had the makings of an empire here? Perhaps it wasn't too late to entice her into some kind of partnership? Together, we could produce a dummy edition of the book, one made up of little more than a cover and a gruesome illustration, a version designed to do nothing more than allow girls the world over to sit in bars alone, unmolested . . .

My favorite line in *Castration and the Heavenly Kingdom* also serves as a succinct summary of the book itself: "The Skoptsy are difficult to love." I could understand why people felt that way, and yet for some reason *I* didn't find the Skoptsy difficult to love at all. True, mine was a love tinged with pity and muddled with horrified fascination—a cloudy, caipirinha kind of love. I loved the Skoptsy because they were creative free-thinkers. Unwilling to accept the strictures of the Russian Orthodox Church, they demonstrated a very bootstrappy, can-do attitude by simply inventing their own religion from scratch. Then, instead of just running about and proclaiming their weirdness, the Skoptsy quietly became successful farmers and traders, well known for their sobriety and diligence. Unwittingly, I found myself considering the benefits of self-castration. Didn't all of us have certain urges we wished we could just walk away from? I started to think about what I might accomplish if, for example, I wasn't so distractible, so easily scuttled by things like castrati research. Having banished physical desire, the Skoptsy in Bucharest were able to apply their newly acquired laser focus to cornering the horse-powered cab market. The possibilities, in other words, were endless.

But dedicated as the Skoptsy might have been to their cause, it was not difficult to poke holes in their theology. Even as far back as 1819, the first tract Tsar Alexander I commissioned to discredit the Skoptsy did a pretty good job by pointing out their failure "to realize that evil inhabits not the body but the soul." The Skoptsy clung to some obscure bits of scripture to justify their antigenitalia stance, and pointed to Origen, an early Christian father who was supposedly castrated, as a role model, but all in all, I tended to agree with the tsar. Wasn't it kind of cheating to just lop off one's offending parts and sashay right up to Heaven? Moreover, even if the Skoptsy *were* right about castration as a means of purification, the question remained, why stop at the privates? I mean, what about one's covetous eyes and troublemaking mouth? Why weren't fingers, which are very versatile and potentially evil appendages when you stop to consider them, included in the toolkit of sin? Maybe it was this failure to think through all the details that made the Skoptsy so endearing to me. After all, I too was a person resistant to analytic thinking and prone to making reckless decisions. And yet, becoming a Skopets was not like buying an armless mannequin at a sidewalk sale or trying out for a strip club in Pigalle on a dare. Becoming a Skopets is forever. You cannot hit Control-Z. You can't undo. And because I had a keen sense of my own capacity to get very excited about something and then make irreversible, potentially disastrous decisions, when I considered the Skoptsy I did not feel at all self-righteous. Instead I thought: There but for the grace of God go I.

Eventually biology and the unforgiving march of progress wore the Skoptsy down. After the Russian Revolution, they found themselves stranded in an atheist country increasingly hostile to the quaint sectarian holdouts of the previous regime. Thwarted by their inability to procreate and saddled with a membership requirement many would consider a nonstarter, the Skoptsy vanished sometime in the 1930s. The final nail in their coffin was delivered in a series of show trials, punctuated by testimony from creepy Soviet outfits like the League of the Militant Godless. The demise of a self-castrating sect was clearly inevitable, but still, I found the news hard to accept. Because if they were truly gone, it meant that I would never fulfill my new dream, which was to hear the Skoptsy sing.

It was a mindless goal I'd developed after reading the Skoptsy were highly musical, their religious ceremonies filled with fervent hymn-singing. I couldn't help fantasizing about the vanished Skopets choirs, even picturing myself joining in on a hymn or two. The lyrics to their songs had survived, but the music itself was gone, and it was only the marriage of the two that I believed would create a perfect window into the Skopets soul, a companion guide to their punishing quest for purity. Perhaps there was still some chance, though—all I really needed was one, last, Google-searchable Skopets to form a duo. If there were any Skoptsy still left out there, I figured, they were sure to have an email address, a blog, at the very least, a book agent. But "Eunuch" did not turn up on anybody's Facebook profile; there were no Skoptsy Meetups in my neighborhood. Searching @skoptsy yielded nothing on Twitter. My quest was dragging on and I was no closer to singing with a Skopets than I was to becoming one myself. Strangely, it was then, just as I was about to concede and rejoin the twenty-first century, that I came across an intriguing piece of new information.

The Skoptsy traced their origins back to an early spiritual Christian prophet by the name of Danila Filippovich. He was a peasant from Kostroma, a mystic wanderer and committed pacifist who fled the Russian army in 1654. While Filippovich was on the lam, he experienced a religious revelation and declared himself a "living god." Despite the fact he preached a radical gospel of self-denial, his following grew rapidly. Of course the tsarist regime eventually took notice of Filippovich's popularity and exiled him to Siberia. Filippovich's teachings ended up forming the core of Skoptsy theology, but he also influenced a number of other sectarians, including some who eschewed the harsh asceticism in favor of his more huggable practices: nonviolence, honesty, brotherly love, vegetarianism, and song-based worship. There was one such group in particular that caught my interest. They were called the Doukhobors, and unlike the Skoptsy and many other religious dissenters, they avoided being stamped out by the Soviets. Despite torture, exile, and dispossession, the Doukhobors managed to survive. But I was even more intrigued when I learned why.

It was because they were *here*. In Canada.

I discovered that aside from a shared love of singing, the Doukhobors, the Skoptsy, and I all had another thing in common, and that thing was Kharkov—a place we all once called home and that we all left in exile. Apparently the Ukrainian province where

I was born had a long history of forcing the independent-minded to flee. My parents tell me that part of the reason we ended up leaving the Soviet Union as political refugees was that the Kharkov branch of the KGB was particularly nasty. I asked my father once why he thought that was and he replied, because they are assholes. It was like he had identified the Kharkov KGB on some Douchebag Table of Elements. "Because they are carbon," he might well have said.

Kharkov gave both the Doukhobors and the Skoptsy their own endless share of trouble. Mass arrests in a major Skopets settlement in Kharkov Province resulted in a famous trial, news of which even made it into *The New York Times*. "Skoptsy Members on Trial," read the headline on October 13, 1910: "Russia Trying Hard to Suppress an Extraordinary Sect." Noting Russia as "a country of strange religious associations," the article described the trial of "141 adherents of the eunuch sect, including 67 women . . ." Remarkably, many of these Skoptsy were eventually acquitted, for while there was no physical doubt the defendants may have been a few fries short of a Happy Meal, there was little proof as to the cause of their disfigurement. Most simply denied membership in the sect and blamed their missing genitalia on . . . something else. One swore his injury was caused by a horse. Another claimed he'd accidentally blundered into a scythe. A third insisted a knife-wielding weirdo attacked him while he was guarding a melon field. (You know, those thieves who start out hankering for some fresh melons, but spontaneously decide a detached penis might do just as well.) The defendants used fire, childbirth, and war as fig leaves for their injuries. A few even opted for a hey-these-things-happen approach, claiming they had no idea where their privates had ambled off to. Eventually, a handful of unrepentant Skoptsy were found guilty and exiled to Siberia, the Haight-Ashbury of the Russian empire.

The Doukhobors were similarly scorned and driven out of Kharkov. They first appeared in the province sometime in the 1730s and endured persecution, then exile, throughout the latter half of the 1700s, until Alexander I issued an edict pardoning them. Alas, the tsar's gesture did nothing to change the attitudes of the Doukhobors' neighbors in Kharkov. When the first group of exiles returned, the villagers at the way station of Saltovo-Ternovo refused to let them into their homes. Their long-awaited homecoming consisted of being forced to stand in a field for more than twenty-four hours. The harassment only continued from there—landlords refused to rent to them, villagers accused them of heresy, and the district authorities persisted in interrogating and imprisoning them. Eventually, the tsar forcibly relocated the dissenters to a patch of land in the fancifully named Milky Waters region at the outskirts of the Sea of Azov. And like my family, once removed from Kharkov, the Doukhobors thrived. They cultivated the land, lived communally, and built a parish center that was given the prophetic name Patience. It was their golden era. But just because the Doukhobors had managed to create some measure of stability and order in their lives did not mean that anyone else found them either stable or orderly. The spring of 1819 marked a new chapter for the Doukhobors—the beginning of their complicated relationship with the West.

The Doukhobors were often referred to as "Russian Quakers" because of their pacifist beliefs. So it was no great surprise when two bona fide members of the Society of Friends made their way to the village of Patience. One was William Allen, a well-to-do English scientist and philanthropist. The other was the French missionary Stephen Grillet. But despite their shared commitment to nonviolence, the Doukhobors differed from the Quakers in almost every respect. Allen and Grillet both found the Doukhobors guilty of extreme vagueness. According to Allen's diary, the trouble began when they asked the Doukhobors to explain their religious practices:

> [W]e wished to know from themselves what were their religious principles. It soon appeared, however, that they have no fixed principles; there was a studied evasion in their answers, and though they readily quoted texts, it is plain they do not acknowledge the authority of scripture, and have some very erroneous notions . . . My spirit was greatly affected, and I came away from them much depressed.

Grillet was similarly dismayed:

> They however stated unequivocally, that they do not believe in the authority of the Scriptures. They look upon Jesus Christ in no other light than that of a good man. We inquired about their mode of worship. They said they met together to sing some of the Psalms of David . . . an old woman . . . began by singing what they call a Psalm; the other women joined in it; then the men . . . each bowed down very low to one another . . . then the old woman, in a fluent manner, uttered what they called a prayer, and their worship concluded; but no seriousness appeared over them at any time . . . We left them with heavy hearts and returned to Altona.

Before leaving, though, Allen and Grillet begged the Doukhobors to recognize the sanctity of the scriptures and the divinity of Jesus. This entreaty was met with blank stares. The Doukhobors believed that the spirit of God already existed within all living things, which is why they abhorred violence and saw no need for icons or church hierarchies. To the straitlaced Quakers, the

Doukhobors' religious ceremonies resembled a tailgate party; to the Doukhobors, the practice of psalm singing was regarded as deeply spiritual—the commingling of voices a means of purification and communing with God. The Quakers left Russia confused and disappointed by the Doukhobors. The Doukhobors remembered the Quakers' visit fondly for decades.

And yet years later, when the Doukhobors were once again subject to torture and exile—this time for disobeying tsarist military orders to take up arms against the neighboring Armenians—the Quakers would be instrumental in helping them leave Russia. In the late 1890s the revered author Leo Tolstoy, also well known as a devout Christian and pacifist, learned of the Doukhobors' plight. He was so deeply moved that he donated all the profits from the publication of his novel *Resurrection* to helping them emigrate to Canada. Much of the remainder of their passage was funded by the Quakers.

I was also moved by the Doukhobors, who believed many of the same things I did, but were ever so much better at it. Was I not also a singing vegetarian originally from Kharkov Province? Yet when confronted with a moral decision no weightier than a hot bowl of *tom yum kung* with a tasty piece of shrimp floating in it, my lofty convictions quickly melted away. Without a dorsal nerve cord or a cerebral cortex, can this decapod crustacean really feel pain? I would ask myself, the first steaming spoonful already halfway to my mouth. And while I could never quite fully commit my life to music, the Doukhobors sang with the full-throated passion of true conviction. They sang as they prayed. They sang as they toiled in the fields. They sang as they burned their guns in protest. They even sang as they were buried in pits up to their necks and tortured to death. They may not have believed in churches or priests or sacraments of any kind, but they did believe in singing. One of the earliest known Doukhobor psalms reads like a manifesto for a musical revolution: "Singing of Psalms is an adornment to our souls . . . It is like the grace of the saints; it adds to one's faith, hope, and love; it covers one with light like the sun. It cleanses one with the water, it burns one's sins like fire, it covers one with holy oil. It puts the devil in one to shame and makes one aware of God."

Dimly I recalled that transcendent time when singing was something that lifted me out of my body, saving me from the grim march of calendar pages and the dark thoughts that come at you in those lonely little anterooms where the mail is collected. In high school, I remember skipping lunch every week to sneak off to empty classrooms so that I could sing by myself. I was always singing back then; in elevators, on subways, walking down the street. But how long ago had that been? Long before I started giving public performances for strangers in exchange for sixty dollars and a pair of drink tickets. Before I learned the countless superficial reasons not to sing, reasons like "this monitor is crackly" or "I'm afraid your cheap microphone has given my mouth an unpleasant little shock for the last time." I wasn't always singing now. I was on the internet. I was spending a lot of time in cars, trying to avoid death-by-Italian. Reading about the Doukhobors singing, I felt more than a twinge of guilt. And jealousy. I performed regularly, and yet somehow they made me miss singing.

Perched on the second floor of a nondescript apartment just a stone's throw away from the Brooklyn-Queens Expressway, I retreated ever further from the outside world and deeper into my Doukhobor scholarship. In the space of a few months, idle curiosity had clearly given way to something more scary that involved the analysis of hospital registers, census results, and burial records from cemeteries no longer on any map. Cobbling together my sixty-page time line of Doukhobor history was a fun time-waster, but all the nights curled up with tomes such as *Russia's*

Lost Reformation: Peasants, Millennialism, and Radical Sects in Southern Russia and Ukraine, 1830–1917 left me longing for more of a human connection with my chosen subject of study. So one day, I wrote to the Doukhobor Discovery Center in Castlegar, British Columbia, and ordered a double album of Doukhobor music on vinyl, *Write it unto thine heart, Herald it with thine lips.* At the same time, I also discovered an extensive library of Doukhobor recordings online, and suddenly I was off, like a delirious child caught in a rainstorm, stomping through the puddles of the Doukhobor song archive. Hits like "We Shall Use Shovels to Work the Land Instead of Taking Up Arms" and "It Was in the Caucasus Mountains That a Great Event Took Place" quickly became the new soundtrack to my morning routine.

I have to say there was a great relief in this. A dozen important music websites were out there, pulsating softly on the internet, promising to give me all the new news and teach me how I might love all the music other people loved. But secretly, they only made me anxious. It was as though a thousand tiny voices were screaming at once: Loud guitars are good! But only if you play them through a bass amp! Never mind, keyboards are good! Or glockenspiels? Have you considered exchanging your drummer for an MC-505? Have you considered dressing exclusively in gold lamé tracksuits? It was exhausting. I felt better here, among this group of matronly women striding across a muddy field on the cover of *Write it unto thine heart, Herald it with thine lips.* Each was dressed in the traditional Doukhobor costume of Georgia and each was carrying a cheap plastic bag—I could even make out the clear outline of a pie tin in one of them. When I looked into their eyes, people who had never heard of a Roland 505 Groovebox looked back at me.

Without quite noticing it, I began to absorb the lilting melodies of the Doukhobors' mournful music, to unconsciously slip

into Doukhobor song myself. Like one day during a companion-
able stroll with Josh down Clinton Street in Brooklyn, when I
began softly keening:

"Volya dukhobortsev, vooolya deeeeket leeeeeyt."

"What is *that*?" asked Josh, a distinct note of alarm sound-
ing in his voice.

"What? Oh *that*! That's the Doukhobor 'Hymn of Hardship.'
Quite an earworm, isn't it?" And I started up again.

"Volya dukhobortsev, vooolya deeeeket leeeeeyt."

"Well, sing the whole song then," Josh said. "You can't just
go on repeating the same line."

This was quite a sensible request, but I'd had a hard time
making out all the words in the Doukhobor dialect and managed
to learn only the beginning of the chorus. So instead I launched
into an English number that the Kootenay Doukhobor Youth
Choir had presented to the United Nations in 1988.

"Tooooooooooil and peeeeeeeeacefoool liiiiiiiiiife," I hollered.

"Oh my God, what is *that*!!!" Josh stopped and stared at me.
A woman walking her dog in front of us had turned to look
around. Even the brownstones looked dismayed.

"It's called 'Toil and Peaceful Life.'" I had to admit the song
sounded much worse without the four-part harmony. "That's the
Doukhobor motto!"

"I would settle for toil and peaceful *wife*," Josh muttered.

And yet, a few weeks later, when he began making arrange-
ments to give a talk in Vancouver, home to the world's largest
Doukhobor research archive, Josh was happy to learn I had a
good excuse to come along. I had fondled the holdings of the
University of British Columbia Doukhobor Research Collection
electronically from afar, downloading soil-classification maps
of Doukhobor lands and theses on the generative phonology of

Doukhobor conjugation, and was dying for a chance to peruse primary source materials in person. Then a few weeks later, as I was lounging around one evening, enjoying the Kootenay Men's Choir's version of "You Have Fallen as Martyrs in Your Heroic Struggle," I felt a mental tug, my forgotten dream to hear the Skoptsy sing surfacing like some distant Oz on the horizon. And then came the epiphany: the Skopsty may be gone, but the Doukhobors were still alive. *And they were still singing.* Through the Union of Spiritual Communities of Christ website, I dug up contact information for the Kootenay Men's Choir and fired off a message. A few days later, a friendly reply came from a man named Elmer Verigin, who offered to arrange a meeting with some fellow choir members. Could it be possible that I was actually going to meet a direct descendant of Peter "Lordly" Verigin, the famous Doukhobor leader who'd inspired Tolstoy and helped the Doukhobors reach Canada? *No,* Elmer replied. *My grandfather was the seventh son of Wasyl Slastukin in Georgia. He became an orphan after his father was kicked by a horse and died. My surname is an adopted one.*

But by the time I received his reply it didn't matter—I had already booked my flight.

The UBC archives turned out to be a two-and-a-half-hour walk from my hotel, but I didn't know that yet when I crossed the Burrard Street Bridge and stopped for a breather at Kitsilano Beach to enjoy the view of the North Shore Mountains, Vancouver shimmering across the bay. I was heading back to the road when an odd little plaque tacked to a wooden pole caught my attention. It featured a black-and-white photograph of a man in a bathing suit, jumping into a swimming pool while clutching what appeared to be a giant propeller. The text below the photo was

taken from an interview with a former lifeguard of Kitsilano
Pool, Ted Luckett, who in March of 1944 was offered two dollars by a local inventor to test his latest invention, the Gyrochute.
The Gyrochute looked like a desiccated daisy, three long blades
jutting from the top of a skinny pole. It was designed to help
people jump to safety from the upper floors of burning buildings, because the fire truck ladders of the day couldn't reach high
enough. But as the photograph attested, the experiment failed.
Luckett did not miraculously glide across the waves; he fell like a
bucket of concrete, Gyrochute in tow.

As I resumed my endless walk to the Doukhobor archive, the
story of the Gyrochute weighed heavily upon me. It seemed like a
metaphor for so many things, perhaps even life itself. We all have
our burning buildings, I mused, and we all create our own Gyro-
chutes in hopes of escaping them, often only to find ourselves
driven downward ever deeper and faster instead. The question
kept gnawing at me: Were the Doukhobors my Gyrochute? By
clinging to them, what kind of Little Odessa was I hoping to
parachute into? Was I hoping to find some piece of home out
there in Castlegar, a kind of Russian oasis? Not like the *real*
Russia—my grandmother's Russia with its uneven stairs and
gallows humor, its kitchens decked in floral wallpaper reeking
of fried meat. Or today's Russia, with its mirrored everything,
throbbing casinos, and bruised self-esteem. But rather some Gol-
dilocks version—a Russia that was "just right." Perhaps unwittingly, I was imagining Castlegar as a place where the Doukhobors
had filtered out all the things I didn't like about the other, more
complicated Russias. Better still, it would be filled with people
like me, people who liked to sing. People whose Russian was heavily
accented and grammatically creative. People who had absorbed
enough North American friendliness to not finger a person's arm
flab upon first being introduced. In Castlegar the Doukhobors
would never make soup broth the way my grandmother had, by

boiling a giant chicken leg for hours, then saving the bones to suck out the marrow. No, they had long ago ditched the greasy, starchy, meat-heavy cuisine of the old country and replaced it with light dill-and-mushroom-laced alternatives. Perhaps the Doukhobors themselves would turn out to be light dill-and-mushroom-laced alternatives to the dark, intimidating Russian intellectuals I'd known as a child! Or to my own self, for that matter.

And yet I feared things wouldn't really turn out that way. More than that, I feared they wouldn't turn out at all. My plans for meeting up with the Doukhobors had gotten a little sketchy. Before leaving for Vancouver, I'd sent a couple of emails to the members of the Kootenay Men's Choir, trying to pin down an exact time and place to meet. I'd heard nothing back, so I decided to give Elmer a call. Only I'd caught him at a bad time.

"Is this Elmer?" I'd asked.

"Are you calling to inquire about the show units?" came a clipped voice in reply.

"Um, no, this is Alina Simone calling. I'm interested in the Doukhobors? I wrote to you earlier? About meeting up with some members of the men's choir?" There was a pause on the other end and suddenly I felt a little ridiculous.

"I'm in the middle of a business meeting right now," said Elmer. "Try calling back later."

And that was it. Too embarrassed to call again, I'd heard nothing more from the Doukhobors since. And now, here I was in Canada.

It was nervousness about the fading prospects for my trip to Castlegar that convinced me to let Nate come along. Nate was a graduate student who lived in a trailer park in Spokane, Washington. For the past few years, he'd made a point of driving out to Portland or Seattle to see me play whenever I toured through. Sometimes we would grab a veggie burrito together before the show. Not long before I left for Vancouver, Nate had dropped me a line and I'd written back mentioning my upcoming trip to Castlegar. Spokane wasn't too far from Castlegar, Nate replied. Maybe he could come along? He would bring a car so I wouldn't have to rent one, and he could help with taping interviews. Now, some people might question the wisdom of agreeing to a road trip with a person you've spent, tops, three hours with. Yet a week before my visit to Castlegar, the prospect of driving through rural Canada alone in search of imaginary Doukhobors suddenly seemed worse.

I received two messages the night before my flight to Castlegar. The first was from Nate. He was spending the night at his mother's place in Sandpoint, Idaho, ready to leave for the Canadian border "at first light," and he wanted to know whether I would like a hand-painted Ukrainian Pysanky egg. The second was from Harold, one of the elusive Doukhobors. He told me that three of them, including Elmer, would meet my flight at the airport tomorrow. I hadn't given the Doukhobors any flight information, but the Castlegar airport wasn't exactly JFK. There was only one morning flight from Vancouver.

Early the next day, I boarded an overwing prop plane that resembled a toy, the kind powered by pulling a string in the back. It was a short flight and before long we were puttering out over the Selkirk Mountains and then down into them. The largest remaining Doukhobor settlements were located in the Kootenays, a rural region that stretched above the Washington-Idaho border. Peter Verigin had named this territory Dolina Ooteshenia, the Valley of Consolation, because it resembled the Doukhobors' lost homeland in the Caucasus. Nonetheless, from 26,000 feet, the laser-cut mountains edged with snow seemed anything but consoling. I could only imagine how they looked to the initial settlers, when this place was little more than a whistle-stop on the Canadian Pacific Railway. But at least the Doukhobors knew something of the life that awaited them after their hard years of farming untamed land. I knew nothing of what awaited me below, aside from Nate, three Doukhobors, and an egg.

When I arrived in Castlegar, Nate was at the gate. He waved happily at me through the glass-paned wall as I wheeled my bag across tarmac that was once the communal property of the Doukhobors.

"Where's my egg?" I demanded as soon as I'd passed through the doors.

"Out in the truck," said Nate, his hand dropping to his side. That's all we had time for. Over his shoulder I saw them waiting— three men well into middle age with a somewhat weatherbeaten look, anxiously scanning the fast-thinning crowd.

I went over and introduced myself, Nate in tow. The Doukhobors were Elmer, Harold, and Harold. They suggested we take a seat at the airport café for some coffee, so I wheeled my bag about five paces from the gate and we all settled down at a table. I pulled out my notebook, which after three days in the UBC Doukhobor archives had accumulated a lot of questions. In particular, I was nagged by the discrepancy between the anthropologist Mark Mealing's claim that Doukhobor psalm-singing was related to Jewish musical traditions, and the ethnomusicologist Kenneth Peacock's description of Doukhobor psalmistry as "a polyphonic development of the znamenny chant." Which hypothesis was closer to the truth? I opened my mouth to ask the question, but then the Doukhobors began to talk. They were plain-spoken men with practical trades—an engineer, a factory worker, a machinist at the pulp mill. Elmer had grown up on a farmstead in Saskatchewan. His father spoke only Russian, so Elmer would claim his school report cards were surveys from the Department of Statistics requesting information about how many chickens they had. One of

the Harolds had grown up in a village where the Sons of Freedom, the most radical of the Doukhobor sects, had burned
schoolhouses and protested against the Canadian government in
the nude; the other was the son of a hard-rock miner who had
died of silicosis. I quietly shelved my questions about the relationship of Doukhobor folklore to that of the Lusatian Sorbs.

Here were stories I wouldn't find in any archive. I hadn't
known that the Doukhobors in Saskatchewan almost sent a
Communist member of Parliament to Ottawa, nor that the Soviets had tried to infiltrate the Doukhobor community in the Kootenays, sending covert representatives to their meetings. I had
heard nothing about the Doukhobor pacifist efforts to support
the Japanese interned by the Canadian government during World
War II. Or about the roadblocks police set up along the highway
so they could search the cars of anyone whose name ended with
"in" or "off." Elmer told of the night when Sons of Freedom radi-
cals blew up an electrical pylon on the shore of Kootenay Lake to
protest government pressure to assimilate, bringing down the region's power grid. With the nearby mines filling with water and
lives in danger, the atmosphere in the nearby city of Nelson turned
mutinous. Taverns filled with wild-eyed men threatening to grab
their guns, go up to the Freedomite village of Krestova, and start
lynching Doukhobors.

"But you must be hungry after that flight," one of the Harolds interrupted. "How about some borscht?"

I looked up from my scribbling and realized that I was a little
hungry. Nate looked eager as well.

"That would be nice, actually," I said, and started gathering
my things, thinking we might hit the legendary Weezy's Borscht
Hut in downtown Castlegar. But Harold simply walked up to the
counter at the airport café and returned holding two steaming
bowls and some slices of homemade bread.

"They sell borscht at the *airport*?" I asked, slack-jawed.

"Doukhobor borscht," replied Elmer, matter-of-factly. "See that lady?" he said, pointing to the sandy-haired woman behind the counter.

"She's a Doukhobor too. And a hell of a good right-fielder. Used to play on my ball team."

I stared down at my soup while Nate dug in. As delightful as all of this was, there was still the fact that I didn't like to eat things that came out of airports. Not even borscht. Not even from Doukhobor airports. Also, my borscht standards were unreasonably high, having been raised on a Ukrainian version my mother prepared according to an old family recipe. Hers was a mind-bendingly delicious thing that took half a day to prepare. I can still remember Mama sweating in front of her ancient cauldron, a pot that looked as though it had been hammered together by elves in the Carpathian Mountains, turning twenty pounds of soup with a heavy spoon and mumbling something about her aching back while Papa and I breezed in and out of the kitchen for a taste.

But my fear of flinging an insult into the face of Russian hospitality was even greater than my fear of airport soup. Whenever I brought home a guest who didn't clean their plate, my mother referred to them forever as Melissa-Who-Did-Not-Like-My-Beef-Stroganoff-with-Mayonnaise.

"It's good," Nate said, nodding.

I smiled queasily at the Doukhobors and took a sip. It *was* good. And not just in a this-won't-give-you-salmonella kind of way. The soup was truly good. And the bread was even better.

When we finished, I realized that a couple of hours had somehow gone by. The Doukhobors had to get back to work, but one of the Harolds asked whether tomorrow we'd like to take a tour of the Cultural Centre in Brilliant followed by a trip to Peter "Lordly" Verigin's tomb. We exchanged phone numbers and stepped outside onto the passenger pickup strip in front of the airport to say our goodbyes. But suddenly the Doukhobors seemed to hesitate. Elmer bent his head and Harold said something too low for me to hear. The other Harold nodded and consulted a crumpled piece of paper pulled from his breast pocket. Then the three of them formed a little line. Elmer cleared his throat.

"Our counter bass went and passed away on us, so we're not in top form. But we'd like to sing a song for you."

The sun was burning brightly over Castlegar and Brilliant and the Valley of Consolation. It was the kind of squinting light that usually fills me with a desperate longing for a windowless room and a strong cup of coffee, but now I blinked into it joyfully. The Doukhobors were *singing*—long mournful notes, rising and falling, in three-part harmony. They sang in a language that was neither exactly Russian nor Ukrainian, accented by a flat twang reminiscent of the midwestern plains. It was an unfamiliar cadence, like something from that other world, that place where the Skoptsy sail across the sky in their ark of salvation. When they finished, Nate and I clapped and begged for another song, and then another. The Doukhobors obliged us, not minding the occasional harried passenger wheeling by with a sideways glance.

After the third song, one of the Harolds jiggled his keys in one hand by way of goodbye. He set off in search of his car just as Elmer turned to me.

"Now how about *you* sing *us* a song?"

"Yeah, you should sing them something," said Nate. "You could do that Russian one."

"Hey, Harry, come back!" called one Harold to the other. "She's gonna sing something for us."

With the Doukhobors assembled before me I turned to face the airport parking lot. Cars came and went. I could see the heat rising from the tops of Mazdas and Ford pickups. A sedan pulled up behind us and a family began loudly unloading bags from their trunk. Somewhere behind me planes lifted off into the mountains.

"*To ne veter vetku klonit,*" I sang in Russian. *'Tis no wind that's bending the branch.* It was an old folk song, the only one I happened to know by heart.

The first notes sounded uncertain, wobbly—I hoped to do better with the second line. I could see Nate from the corner of my eye, fiddling with his iPhone. And there were Harold, Harold, and Elmer, watching me expectantly from their place under the awning. I found it hard to concentrate, to forget that I happened to be standing in an airport parking lot, hot under the extra sweater that wouldn't fit into my suitcase, my lungs full of exhaust and asphalt fumes. I closed my eyes for a moment, tried to clear my mind, concentrate. And then, without warning, there it was. The adornment. That feeling of grace the Doukhobors knew well, that can come over you in the most ordinary of places, even as you confront a group of strangers. The thing you are trying to do—to turn air into notes, and notes into song—seems as ridiculous and impossible as an alchemist's trick. You feel leaden, earthbound. Your audience looks at you, their faces inscrutable. You close your eyes and focus on the melody. You hold it there in your mind, trying to pin it into place. But it is like trying to pin a living butterfly to a board. You steady yourself again. You take another deep breath. This is pointless. You open your mouth and hope for the best.

And then something catches. And then you soar.

Mama's Borscht Recipe

Ingredients

    2 tablespoons vegetable oil
    1 medium onion, finely minced (about 1 cup)
    1 medium carrot, peeled and finely shredded
    1 small (or ½ medium) beet, peeled and finely shredded

half of a 6-ounce can tomato paste
about 3 liters of water
salt and black pepper
4–5 large potatoes, peeled and cut into cubes
2 medium-large green bell peppers, cored, seeded, and cut
    into ½-inch squares
1 small (or ½ medium) head green cabbage, finely shredded
2 cloves garlic, chopped (optional)
basil or 2 bay leaves (optional)
juice of 1 lemon (to taste—optional)
2–3 teaspoons sugar (to taste—optional)

Directions

Heat the oil in a large skillet (6 quarts) over medium-high heat until hot. Reduce the heat to medium, add the onion, and cook, stirring occasionally, until golden brown, about 10 minutes. Add carrot and beet, cook just until they start to change color. Add the tomato paste and cook together, stirring, for 5 minutes.

Meanwhile, simmer water and 1¾ teaspoons salt in a large soup pot. Stir in the fried vegetables with tomato paste, bring to a boil. Add potatoes, green peppers, cabbage, and garlic; simmer over low heat until potatoes are tender (about 20 minutes). Season to taste with salt and pepper.

Add bay leaves or basil (optional). Bring to a boil again and simmer covered over very low heat for another 35–45 minutes. Add more water if needed. Adjust the taste with lemon juice and sugar according to personal preferences.

Makes 14 to 16 servings. May be served garnished with sour cream for individual portions.

Keep in mind: borscht tastes better the next day (and even better the next week).

TAKE OFF YOUR PANTS
AND DRINK WITH US

Not a single trip that I've ever taken to Siberia—and there have been many—has ever gone according to plan. Perhaps that's why I have such an irrational appreciation for these first crumpled hours. Landing. Luggage. Cab. Hotel. Thank you very much, Siberia. Everything will go to shit soon enough, but at least you've eased me into things by way of this boring but reassuringly logical progression of events. And let me just start out by saying that the landing strip at Tolmachevo in Novosibirsk is not a series of rotting planks laid across the snow, and that today, the airport is neither an igloo nor some deteriorating Soviet bunker. It is the same citadel of gleaming steel and polished glass you find in any Western city. Oh, and you will not implode upon first contact with the atmosphere. Your eyeballs will not shatter. Frost will not instantly form on your underpants. To be honest? It's really not *that* cold. You will be comforted to find no fewer than five cafés happy to sell you an overpriced cheese sandwich and a cappuccino with almond syrup at seven in the morning. See? Just like everywhere else. Aside from the icicles dangling from the awnings like a row of loaded Kalashnikovs, you'd think you'd just landed in Missoula or Bar Harbor.

By now, I've become something of a scholar when it comes to arriving in Novosibirsk. For example, I can tell you that the cab-drivers greeting arrivals to Tolmachevo can be divided into exactly two groups. The first is represented by a young man with closely cropped hair, a black leather jacket, and a vaguely thuggish air. He has no interest in talking and will spend the whole ride blaring *blatnaya muzika* from the car stereo while keeping his eyes tethered to the backsides of blondes making their miraculous way over the ice in stiletto heels. The other kind of cabdriver requires far more energy. He is slightly dumpy, with the collective sorrow of the gulag puddled in his drooping eyes. Kind of a Siberian version of Bill Murray. I will enter the cab and automatically reach for the seat belt only to find that the clasp has either been sawed off with great violence or shoved so deep into the anus of the car that, with my mere arm's-length grasp, I could never hope to retrieve it. Then the cabbie and I will exchange introductions and have a conversation that roughly follows this script:

CABBIE: So . . . America. How is it?

ME: Good, uh, pretty good. How's life in Siberia?

CABBIE: Eh—how is *life*? Life is hard. Life is hard everywhere. Where in America do you live? Virginia?

ME: I live in New York.

CABBIE: Ah! My sister-in-law's nephew is studying at the polytechnic institute in Virginia. Perhaps you know Bulat Antipovich?

ME: Sorry. New York is pretty far from Virginia.

CABBIE: What a pity. He is an exemplary young person. Tell me, how much does it cost to rent an apartment in New York?

ME: That depends.

CABBIE: But approximately?

ME: Really, it depends on exactly where you live and what kind of apartment you have.

CABBIE: Who cares, right? It is all the same now anyway—
New York, Moscow, Novosibirsk—everywhere is equally expensive, *blyad*.

ME: True.

(There is a pause punctuated only by the sound of cheesy
pop music from a generic radio station.)

CABBIE: I hate this music. Phoo! Everything on the radio
these days is carrot-love.

(You have no idea that in Russian *carrot-love* is an idiom for
love-shmove. *Shmove* doesn't usually mean "carrot" in Russian,
except in this case, when it does.)

CABBIE: Tell me, what kind of car do you drive?

ME: Honda Civic.

CABBIE: You have automatic transmission or manual?

ME: Manual.

CABBIE: Tsk. Manual is not so good. It is very capricious?

ME: Sometimes.

(Then there is another long pause during which one's attention is called to the motor grinding away like a fork stuck in an
Insinkerator. The morning mist is burning up in the first rays of
sunlight and pale gray outlines of concrete buildings begin to
emerge on the horizon, like illustrations from Dante's *Purgatory*.)

CABBIE: Alina?

ME: Yes, Vanya?

CABBIE: Can I ask you something?

(Pause.)

ME: Sure.

(Pause.)

CABBIE: If there is such a thing as God, why must we endure
such suffering . . . ?

And so it will go until we arrive in Akademgorodok, where
the cabbie will insist on calling his wife to get Bulat's phone

number so that when you get back to New York you can tell him that Vanya wishes him success with his studies and promises that his wife, Raisa, will make his favorite *holodetz*—a frightening kind of jellied meatloaf, the key ingredient of which is commonly cow's feet—when he comes home for the holidays.

With the cab ride behind me, I will stand at the threshold to the Golden Valley Hotel, confronting my final hurdle. Zolotaya Dolina does not look anything like a golden valley. It is a typical Soviet-era hotel, and as such it more closely resembles an egg carton. I approach the front desk full of apprehension. Since the room quality at Golden Valley varies so drastically, the registration process tends to involve a certain degree of negotiation. Once I went to sleep in a room on the third floor and woke up thinking I was on a ski slope. An Arctic wind had made its way across a thousand miles of tundra to find a happy outlet here, in the gap below my windowsill. I had opened the door to my room only to duck down immediately when I discovered real Siberian birds flapping down the length of the entire hallway, cawing ravenously. So now I approach the reception desk with a cut-the-shit look on my face. "Don't even think of putting me on the floor with the birds," my eyes say, "I want to wake up with the ends of my hair fried to a crisp. I want to feel like I am falling asleep under a tanning lamp. I want *heat*. And plenty of it. Because if one thing's for sure, Comrades, it's that I didn't come to Siberia for the weather."

But why did I keep coming back to Siberia? I had no family connection to Siberia and, when I first traveled there, no friends to speak of. The Ukrainian city of Kharkov, where I was born and where my father's family still lives, lies nearly two thousand miles west of Novosibirsk. My parents, and everyone else I knew, wondered why, if I wanted to experience Russia, I didn't just start with

Moscow or St. Petersburg, the cosmopolitan city home to my mother's side of the family. It was as though I was passing up New York City or San Francisco in favor of an extended stay on Three Mile Island. The first time I traveled to Siberia, where the non-profit I worked for ran a teaching program, could have been passed off as a mere professional obligation. But that would have been a roundabout lie. I'd accepted the job to begin with only because of its peculiar regional focus. Besides, that explanation would have withered under the scrutiny of my subsequent trips, which at last count numbered about a dozen. I have spent, all told, about a year living in Siberia. And when I wasn't working or traveling in Siberia, I was thinking about Siberia. I was listening to bootlegs of the Siberian punk singer Yanka Dyagileva or researching the Skoptsy, a castrati sect once banished to the far reaches of Yakutia.

I still don't have a single compelling reason for what first intrigued me about the place, only nebulous justifications and unsatisfying excuses. First there was the notion that Siberia was kind of like Russia, only with training wheels. A good place for beginners. The only taste of Russia I'd ever had was my own family, and that small dose in itself was already overwhelming. I feared I just couldn't handle the big cities of western Russia. What if everyone in St. Petersburg was like my mother and spoke in ALL CAPITAL LETTERS ALL THE TIME? Then there was my admittedly unhealthy fascination with Siberia's weirdness, its monumental scale and inhuman temperatures, its Evenk rein-deer hunters, Tuvan throat singers, and Altai shamans—all things that sounded considerably more interesting than an eight-hour stroll through the Kremlin, quality time with Lenin's petrified corpse notwithstanding. But more than anything, I bought into this mythic idea that Siberia was where you went to experience the *real* Russia. From the first time I crossed the Urals, I remained convinced that it was only here, among the descendants of Cos-sack warriors, political prisoners, and religious dissenters, in these

gray and cosseted cities, that I would become one with the True
Slavic Soul; I would come to terms with the country my family
had fled and deconstruct my own personal issues regarding cultural identity and displacement. Or perhaps I would do none of
these things. Perhaps I would just fill my backpack with birch
tchotchkes and endure some endless train rides. Regardless of
what I did, my parents had me convinced that my first trip to any
part of Russia, however real or fake, would also be my last. Like
most Western immigrants who came of age in the Soviet Union,
they were terrified by news reports from the New Russia, all
those stories of mafia shootouts and pyramid scams and nuclear
warheads being sold for a dollar on eBay. It was a murderous
chaos that had nothing to do with the repressed and stagnant
country they remembered, a place where problems officially did
not exist.

"These people have become complete moral degenerates!"
my parents bleated. "They will do anything for money. They will
kill you for an egg sandwich and send your remains home in a
ziplock bag. So when you are cold and dead, and your kidneys
are up for sale in the back of some newspaper in Cherepovets, do
not blame us. Remember: we warned you about that godforsaken
hole."

Then one day, while I was in college, my roommate's good
friend from high school was murdered while on a language exchange program in Moscow. This event only confirmed what my
parents had already expended vast amounts of spittle trying to
explain. It would take another decade for me to gather up my
courage and travel to Russia. Even then, one could scarcely say I
threw caution to the wind; my first day in Chita City was spent
staring hungrily out the window, wondering whether I should
risk calling a taxi to ferry me safely to the tiny grocery store
across the street. But after several days spent alone in a dorm

room, deep in the drafty confines of the Chita Pedagogical Institute, with nothing but the sounds of mice and cockroaches playing badminton in my kitchen cabinets to keep me company, I
realized that life in Siberia was not a real-world version of *Grand
Theft Auto*. I could stop hugging the sides of buildings whenever
I stepped outside, because if anything was going to kill me, it was
my very own predilection for a particular sort of Siberian smoked
cheese composed of about 90 percent saturated fat and 10 percent
salt. No, my problem with Siberia was not a surplus of excitement but its polar opposite, the age-old dilemma of how to fill all
of that time and space, two things that Siberia had always offered
both tourists and prisoners alike in great abundance.

I felt this most intensely during my longest stay in Siberia, a
five-month stretch during which I worked for a large foundation
based in the city of Novosibirsk. My research assignment actually involved a great deal of travel, but for that first month, I lived
in the city and worked at the main office. I was still too scared to
wander far beyond my comfort zone, so my orbit was limited to
the spheres of home and office, trips to the market, and a daily
quest for coffee that did not emerge, granulated, from a dusty
packet. My self-imposed isolation came to an end only once I left
Novosibirsk for Tomsk and my field research began.

I remember it was my first day off, and I had taken what tourists in warmer climes like to call "the chicken bus" to Kolarovo, a
tiny village where one of the rare eighteenth-century Orthodox
churches to have survived the Soviet wrecking ball still stood.
When I arrived I found that Kolarovo did not disappoint, with its
wooden cottages sinking quietly into the dark earth and its picturesque church keeping watch from a lonely atoll like a Palekh
miniature come to life. After visiting the church I decided to hike
down to a lake I'd spotted in the valley below and was soon walking along the shore, basking in the sight of all that open land and

the boundless, incredible Siberianness of it all. But half an hour later the spell was broken. I was bored, itchy, and feeling the pangs of a caffeine-deprivation headache coming on. Moreover, dusk was falling and I was starting to worry about the bus situation. I hadn't bothered to examine the schedule too closely, figuring that sooner or later a *marshrutka* would putter by. Now, standing by the road and squinting into the darkening distance, I began to doubt this was true.

That's when I noticed two men clambering up the untended path from the lake, swatting the weeds out of their path and cursing as they made their way toward me. When they drew closer I could see that one of them was dressed in jeans and a collared shirt, the other in a dirty Adidas tracksuit.

"*Privet!*" the cleaner of the two called out. He was still huffing when he stopped in front of me. "We were down at the lake and saw you standing by the side of the road for some time now. Just wondering if you might be lost . . . ?" The man in jeans introduced himself as Pasha and his friend as Sasha, grimacing a little at the unfortunate rhyme. They had been fishing, Pasha explained, and grilling shashlik down by the shore when they'd spotted me. I told them I had come from Tomsk and was just wondering about the next bus back, whereupon Pasha confirmed my fears—the last bus had been the one that brought me to Kolarovo.

"Well, you're in luck!" Pasha exclaimed. "I live in Tomsk and can drive you home after dropping Sasha off at his mother's house. My car is only just down the road . . ."

I thought for a moment. There was a part of me that doubted getting into a car with two random men I met by the side of a lake in rural Siberia was such a genius move. Then again, neither was spending the night on the streets of Kolarovo, which were mostly made of dirt. I agreed to come along, and when we reached the car, I was happy to see that the trunk really was filled with fishing gear. But we had been motoring down the lane for only a short time when my qualms surfaced again. I began to notice some other things—specifically things about Sasha, who had settled in the backseat directly behind me. The first was, he stank. The reek of alcohol coming off him was so strong that he may have officially qualified as a solvent. Then, when Sasha leaned forward to paw at Pasha's shoulder, I noticed something else: the blurry tattoos between the knuckles of his left hand—never a good sign in Russia.

"Pasha? Pasha!" Sasha barked. *"Bliad, zayebala menya eta derevnya na huy do polusmerti. Blevat tyanet ot etikh opizdinevshikh starykh zasranok."* This could roughly be translated as "Whore-fuck, this village has dicked me half dead. These old shitty cunts make me wanna puke." Exhausted by this Shakespearean effort, Sasha rolled down the window, horked into the wind, and muttered, "Fuck. I'm thirsty as shit," before using the back of Pasha's seat to rub the spit off his face.

Pasha twisted out from under Sasha's hand and shot me a shrugging kind of look. I managed a weak smile in return while a montage of images unspooled in my mind: the flash of roadside weeds and broken bottles, a grainy close-up of a newspaper headline, my parents awkwardly wiping their ashy fingers on their pants after sprinkling my remains in the little pond behind their house . . .

A few minutes later we were idling outside Sasha's mother's home, where a stout, straw-haired woman with a battered face was stacking firewood in the yard. Sasha leaned heavily on the car door before righting himself and lurching unsteadily toward the house. The woman watched his progress with a pained look, shaking her head sadly. She glanced up and noticed Pasha at the wheel, who rolled down the window and shouted, *"Derzhis,* Marina Sergeievna! *Derzhis!"* The woman only nodded gravely and waved at the car as we pulled away.

"I am sorry," Pasha said. "My friend is a drunk."

"Yes," I affirmed.

"He only just returned to the village after a long time away and doesn't know what to do with himself."

"Where was he?" I asked, full of awareness of where he was.

"Prison."

"What for?"

Pasha glanced at me for a long moment before returning his attention to the road. "He got into a fight at a bar and killed a man."

"How did he kill him?" I blurted, and as these unfamiliar new words left my mouth I had the distinct feeling that I'd somehow misplaced my immediate priorities.

"With his bare hands," he replied.

And then we settled into the awkward silence that usually follows these kinds of revelations. But once the windows were rolled down and the air cleared of its eye-watering fumes, Pasha and I began to talk again. It turned out that he'd grown up in Kolarovo, where he and Sasha had been childhood friends, but was now a successful businessman, running his own furniture factory in Tomsk. The one advantage, so far as I could see, of sharing a long car ride with the friend of a convicted murderer was that I could finally learn something about the seedier side of life in Tomsk. Surely something darker lay behind the lacework shutters of all those quaint wooden houses? Surely there were more interesting things to do than walk the streets in search of a salad without mayonnaise? Pasha saw what I was getting at and, before dropping me off at my hotel, promised to give me a little tour during my stay. After that, I would get a call from him every few days. Would I fancy a trip to a local casino? Perhaps a visit to a nearby Gypsy village well known for drug trafficking? How about a drive down to the place on the highway where prostitutes wait to pick up truckers?

Pasha was about ten years older than me, but he had a pretty wife who was much younger, and a baby. I sensed that his interest in me wasn't prurient, but rather, he just enjoyed having an American around as a weird sort of pet, the way a well-to-do Manhattanite might accessorize herself with an African serval. Regardless of Pasha's motives or his taste in friends, he turned out to be an excellent guide to the underside of Tomsk, and I returned to Novosibirsk a far better informed Siberian citizen. I also found that, for better or worse, my natural defenses were worn away by this experience. The fear of Russia my parents had worked so hard to instill in me was gone, replaced, it seemed, by a newfound thirst for adventure that left me feeling whorish and pretty much up for anything.

I suppose this is what accounted for my presence in the front row of a male strip show on the shore of an artificial sea just outside of Akademgorodok a few weeks later. By then I had managed to make some genuine friends in Siberia, among them Roman, a charming half-Gypsy, half-Chechen musician who supported himself by hosting laser shows at local nightclubs, using equipment lifted from one of the many bankrupt research institutes littering Novosibirsk. The special occasion that night was the arrival of a touring striptease starring "Tarzan," a bodybuilder better known as the husband of the Russian pop singer Natasha Koroleva. To translate this into American terms: imagine going to a club in Umiat, Alaska, to see Céline Dion's husband take his clothes off. It was something like that.

Club Neokom was located on the shore of Beach Neokom; both of them belonging to the Novosibirsk megaconglomerate, Neokom. And although it was hard to imagine anything raunchy or dangerous happening in this soulless place, under the canvas roof of a glorified beer tent blasting carrot-love all over ill-clad women and their thick-necked boyfriends, Roman approached the ticket booth with noticeable trepidation.

"Just be careful," he said, eyeing me warily as I twirled my digital camera by its faux-leather strap. "I can't really keep an eye on you while I'm setting up the laser, and there are fights at this place practically every weekend."

"No prob!" I chirped.

"People have been shot and killed here. Seriously."

"Seriously!" I repeated joyfully, poking him in the arm.

"Tonight's going to be crazy," Roman warned, shaking his head. "And please watch where you point that thing," he added, indicating my camera. "I mean it."

A few minutes later the music cut out for the announcement that the show would begin in ten minutes. Roman wandered off to get some beer and I immediately made for the stage, determined to stake out a spot in the front row. I was resting my elbows on the raised wooden platform, testing the autofocus on my camera, when I felt the firm tap on my shoulder.

"Coo-coo, Alinachka," Roman hissed through his teeth. "What the hell do you think you're doing up here?"

"I'm waiting to see the show—"

"Yeah, you can see the show from the laser booth too," he said, taking me by the elbow.

"Look at me," I whined. "I'm barely five feet tall—do you think I'm really going to be able to see anything back there with you?"

Roman glanced around uneasily. "Listen, I'm going to be running the laser, and if you're not with me, I can't be held accountable."

"Who's holding you accountable?"

"Okay, whatever," Roman called, as he turned and walked away. "Those pictures better be good."

I was too busy trying to puzzle out what had gotten into Roman to pay attention to the announcement that the show was just about to begin. He was hardly the paranoid type, so why the sudden grade-school—WOMP! Both my thoughts and the air in my chest were cut off as my pancreas was mashed into the hard edge of the stage. I was being suffocated by women. Hundreds and hundreds of women, all screaming and filling my vanishing air space with their highly flammable breath. None of them seemed to care that the thing separating them from the object of their desire was not a stack of bricks or a pylon, but an inconveniently fleshy person. A consultant I'd once met in Irkutsk had confessed to me that the most embarrassing thing that had ever happened to her on assignment in Siberia was peeing her pants because she could not traverse a narrow, congested pathway carved into the snow fast enough to reach her hotel. Was I about to surpass this impressive milestone by laying down my life here? At Club Neokom? So that a twenty-three-year-old computer programmer from Berdsk could get six inches closer to Tarzan's tight ass? And my poor family! Sure, they had predicted my death, but what fresh hell of humiliation *this* would turn out to be. Adrenalized, I started elbowing hard, indifferent to where my blows landed until the pressure eased and the lights dimmed.

Really, all Roman had to do if he wanted to get me as far away from the action as possible was explain that Russian strip shows, unlike those in America, included a graphic audience-participation component. My boss, who is fluent in Managementspeak, liked to call revelations like these "learning points." Another learning point for me would have been the news that the front row serves as prime recruiting ground for said graphic audience-participation component. Had I known this, I would have happily volunteered to spend the night in the parking lot, watching the show through binoculars from the van window. Instead I was obliviously clicking away when a freakishly taut man dressed in a police uniform hauled the first woman up on stage. This was not Tarzan but one in a long string of gladiators, firefighters, gymnasts, and sailors brought out to warm up the crowd for the main attraction. I watched as the police officer offered the woman a rose, as he led her around the stage by one hand, as he removed her clothes and then proceeded to do some things that I'm pretty sure a fair number of married couples have never gotten around to. And she was just the first of many willing victims.

Avoiding the rose became my new imperative in life. Every Tarzan mini-me had one. They would prowl the stage, waving it around with a languid motion of the wrist like some mesmerizing wand of shame. Then they would drop dramatically to one knee, extending the rose toward the front row and inducing every woman within reach to claw at one another as if it were a lingerie fire sale at Loehmann's and the last thong on Earth was at stake. Lucky for me there were too many other contenders, all drunk and hollering and flinging their anatomy into the air, for me to attract much notice. Until the very end, that is. Until . . . Tarzan.

I remember there was this palpable shift in the atmosphere, hands tightening around the necks of beer bottles, followed by a cannon blast of carrot-love. Then Tarzan burst onto the stage in a white satin toga, and never in my life had I seen a man who so much resembled a horse. When he threw back his mane of long blond hair I fully expected to hear a long, low braying sound, but instead there was just the roar of the crowd, losing its collective mind. Tarzan cantered into the spotlight and paused dramatically, letting his toga slip to reveal one strategically flexed buttock. The rose was in his mouth, clenched between his teeth. He rearranged his toga again to reveal an aggressively glossy thigh, slid toward the edge of the stage, and pressed what remained of his toga to his prominent crotch with one hand. For a moment he seemed to be locked in some kind of desperate struggle with the crotch, as though a seagull had gotten caught in his G-string and was desperately trying to break free. The woman next to me started screaming so loudly that I feared she might expel a tonsil right there into my beer, and at the sound Tarzan turned his head. But for some reason, his eyes slid right over her and instead landed squarely on me. I immediately dropped my camera to my side and began shaking my head. No, Tarzan, I projected telepathically. This won't be any fun for either of us, I'm afraid. I am really bad at getting publicly molested. The sight of me sobbing hysterically and pathetically slapping at your big, impossible muscles and screaming for Roman to please melt you with his laser will be a total buzzkill for all the nice people who paid three hundred rubles to come here tonight. You totally deserve better. What about the nice lady in that one-piece spandex thingee over there . . . ? I look like a hazmat inspector compared to her. See the way her neck muscles are bulging? I think that means she's really excited to meet you! But Tarzan just stood at the foot of the stage looking down at me, smiling his horsey smile through the rose in his teeth. He turned around and for a second I thought my luck had changed, that he'd decided to seek his next victim elsewhere. But Tarzan didn't move, instead he started tipping his head back, back, ever further back, until he was suspended in a quivering arc right over my head. I was still completely hemmed in on every side, so there was nothing to do but watch as he opened his mouth and the rose fell, head over stem, down toward me.

It was very hard to avoid the impulse to raise my hands and catch the rose, but still, I managed to do so, keeping my arms pressed tight to my sides. Even after the rose hit me, even with hundreds of women watching and Tarzan waiting and the rose sitting weirdly on top of my head where it had gotten stuck in my hair, I remained motionless, hoping that if I pretended like nothing had happened, this whole thing might just quietly blow over. It was useless—immediately the hands of half a dozen women were in my hair, pulling and screeching. I dropped down, screaming and slapping uselessly at the swarm above me. A moment later a woman who'd been standing behind me jumped to her feet, brandishing the rose and whooting like a soccer champion. I barely had time to stand and bring the viewfinder to my face once more in time to catch—

FLASH! Tarzan pulling the woman to his chest with one hand and removing her tank top with the other as—

FLASH! the gladiator, the bullfighter, the cop, and the gymnast emerged from the wings to—

FLASH! surround the woman on all sides, feeding on her like some kind of smut octopus and—

FLASH! doing things that I would feel uncomfortable confessing within the echoing confines of my own subconscious, including—

FLASH! acts that would surely qualify them all for public execution in certain rogue states until—

FLASH! the show ends and the strippers abruptly vanish, leaving her to wander the stage topless like a refugee from a porn shoot whereupon—

FLASH! the M.C. comes out holding a jar of jelly high above his head and announces a competition promising—

FLASH! the couple that can lick the most jelly off each other's body within the next five minutes would win the ultimate prize, namely—

FLASH! *this* cell phone. Brought to you by Neokom.

The night did not end there. It ended only after many different couples had announced themselves to the world wearing nothing but apricot preserves, and a barmaid hit me on the head *hard*

when she discovered me reading *Garri Potter i Filosofskii Kamen*
in a dark corner of the tent, where I had crawled off like a sick
cat in search of a place to die. It truly ended only after two men
got in a fight next to the ticket booth, and with the rising sun
reflecting off pools of their blood, Roman steered me around the
police barricades and back to the van without even having to say
"I told you so."

Looking back, this period was clearly the apex of my obsession
with Siberia, when I greeted even the cheesiest and most repellent
aspects of its culture with the awe, respect, even gratitude, of a
visiting anthropologist. This was before my trips to Siberia began to take on the familiar contours of business travel the world
over, with its wireless-enabled hotels, overpriced salad bars, and
surplus of wood-laminated surfaces. It was still four years before
the weekend I spent locked in a train compartment of the Trans-
Siberian with a family whose matriarch addressed everyone in
the short, angry diction of a Chinese fry cook ("Masha! Slip-
pers! Dinner! Now!"), whose patriarch's body odor was reminiscent of nothing so much as the Red Army trenches circa 1942,
and whose daughter's handheld electronic game emitted an in-
cessant, circuit-breaking BEEP! that called to mind that famous
Communist slogan "Luddites of the World Unite!" This journey
broke me the way alcohol broke Hemingway, Hollywood broke
Capote, and the Vietnam War broke LBJ. When I finally emerged
from this train, in a small city in northern Tyumen Oblast by
the name of Ishim, what little enthusiasm I had left for Siberia,
for befriending strangers and courting adventure in general, was
dead as dust.

But in the summer of 2005, I was still wide-eyed and eager to
experience anything that would impart to me even the thinnest
patina of Russian authenticity. So it was with real excitement

that I arose one morning and set off for the local Laundromat with a few weeks' worth of dirty clothes. My first Siberian Laundromat! And perhaps it was that latent desire to go native that accounted for what happened next, because somehow it tests the bounds of credulity to believe that I, the daughter of Soviet political refugees and a person more than a little impatient (desperate?) to embrace my ancient heritage and lay claim to the corresponding dose of unbearable suffering that was my birthright, just happened to leave my American passport on the bus home *by accident.*

It was only after I had returned to my friend Sarah's flat and started to pack my things for a trip back to Tomsk, where work was sending me on Monday, that I noticed it was missing.

"Sarah. My passport . . ." I began.

Sarah took one look at my face and guessed the rest. "Have you looked everywhere?" she asked, her voice skating up a register.

But I didn't have to look everywhere. I had been traveling around Siberia with the same pack for months now. My hands were like airport X-ray scanners. Besides, in Russia everyone kept their passport on the ready, like a gun in a holster.

"Okay. Don't panic," Sarah said. But hers were the eyes of a ferret that had been set on fire, and the full text of her expression read: "Of course you will miss Josh terribly at first, but don't worry, there are plenty of other fish in the artificial sea! And did I mention that I have a friend who can get you a great deal on a one-bedroom here in Akademgorodok?"

After not panicking together for two claustrophobic hours, we decided to call our friend Konst. Now, Konst is the kind of congenitally optimistic person who remains cheerful even when informed that a horde of bioengineered mosquitoes carrying the Ebola virus is on its way to his apartment. When I told him I'd lost my passport, I expected to hear something like: Bah! Passports are so overrated. Welcome to the underground resistance,

Comrade! But instead, Konst just said, "Duuuude . . ." And then he said nothing. Since Konst lived around the corner from the bus station, I asked whether he minded checking to see whether someone had turned my things in to the dispatcher. He instantly volunteered to go over there at 5:30 in the morning, just as soon as the depot opened. *Now* I really started to panic. Konst was taking this dead seriously. It was not a good sign.

Next we called the American consulate and I had a conversation with an employee of the U.S. government that went something like this.

ME: Hi. I'm an American citizen here in Novosibirsk and I just lost my passport.

THEM: You will need to come to the nearest U.S. consulate to apply for a duplicate, but I have to warn you, the process can take weeks.

ME: Great! Where is the nearest consulate?

THEM: Yekaterinburg.

ME: Okay, but that's over eight hundred miles away . . .

THEM: I'm sorry, you must apply in person at the consulate.

ME: I understand, but without a passport, I can't buy train tickets or plane tickets, I can't stay at a hotel or exchange foreign currency. In fact, legally, I'm not even supposed to go outside without carrying my passport.

THEM: Yes.

ME: Right, so you see, it's a bit of a Catch-22 situation.

THEM: Do you have any idea how serious this is?

ME: I do. But I can't buy a ticket to Yekaterinburg without a passport.

THEM: Yes, well, that's your problem.

ME: Ha! Well, of course it's my problem. I am very well aware of that, *thanks*. It's not like I'm asking you to personally come get me, *thanks*. I just wish someone would explain how the FUCK I am supposed to— Hello?

I stayed up until 5:45 in the morning, when Konst called to say he'd had no luck at the bus station, before finally lying down to contemplate all my parents' prophetic warnings. Somehow, relying solely on my own stupidity and carelessness, with zero assistance from nuclear arms dealers, corrupt bureaucrats, the secret police, or the Red Mafia, I had managed to become a prisoner in Siberia. Would self-satisfaction win out over horror, when I called my parents to tell them their instincts had been right all along? They had told me so and now here I was, doomed to a lifetime of white food. I stared at the ceiling, chastened and miserable. Nothing was so dear to me as the image of my triumphant return to America, wreathed in amber necklaces, quoting Lermontov in accentless Russian while doling out gifts of Khokhloma to my parents like Marie Antoinette. Such was my pride that I vowed right then to say nothing. I would not ask for their help in fixing this mess. Not even if it meant crawling to Yekaterinburg on my elbows, camping in the American consulate's dumpster, and subsisting on mayonnaise-and-potato-peel sandwiches for however long it took.

So one can only imagine the tender feelings I had for the Akademgorodok bus driver who tracked me down to return my bag with passport, credit cards, and not a ruble missing the following day. I knew full well how lucky I was. And as I took all the cash out of my newly returned wallet and pressed it into the palm of a True Slavic Soul, it was with this silent prayer: May it come to pass that the next time you find a foreign passport on your bus, you will do another hapless stranger the same kind turn, so they too might return home safely to their country, perpetuate the lies to their family, and preserve the illusion that all went well with them in Mother Russia.

·

It was on the way to Tomsk that my cell phone rang and I was informed that every hotel in the city was sold out.

"Your room was supposed to have been booked," said the guy at our Tomsk affiliate, "but that did not happen."

I love how in Russia news like this is always delivered in the passive voice, as though it were God's fault my room wasn't booked, and not that of some very specific person by the name of Tatiana or Zhenya who spent the week sitting at her desk experimenting with ringtones. When I arrived in Tomsk, I threw myself at the mercy of the concierge at the hotel next to the train station, who did finally succeed in finding me a bed. It was a share, but I accepted it gratefully.

Upon unlocking the door to my hotel room, I was greeted by two women. The first was Lyudmila, a short blonde with a bad bottle dye job and some teeth issues. She was in her late twenties, but looked closer to forty due to the fact that she was making the most of stage-three alcohol dependency. Lyudmila was my roommate; the other woman turned out to be her friend Sveta. Sveta was the kind of tall, thin, flawless beauty that Siberian backwaters pump out with such miraculous consistency you'd think a Japanese automaker were involved. Lyudmila and Sveta were both bookkeepers who'd come from the northern Siberian city of Nizhnevartovsk for a convention. Was this why every hotel room in the city was booked? I thought to myself. Was Tomsk to bookkeepers what Vegas was to strippers?

After we discussed America and the price of a two-bedroom apartment, the quality of my car, the state of my marriage and my ovaries, I asked Lyudmila and Sveta about Nizhnevartovsk.

"Nizhnevartovsk is the best place on Earth," Lyudmila answered without hesitation.

"Yes. It is very, very rich. We have one of the biggest oil fields in Russia. So residents have excellent facilities—sports complex, theaters, concert halls . . ." Sveta added, "Do you know how much a bookkeeper in Nizhnevartovsk earns per month?"

I had to admit, it wasn't a data point I kept on hand, so Sveta quoted some number of rubles.

"Wow," I said, having no idea whether this was good or bad.

"Yes, wow. And do you know how much a bookkeeper in Tomsk makes?"

I shook my head and here Sveta quoted a much lower number.

"Wow," I repeated, dutifully.

"We also have the Ob River, the most beautiful in all of Russia, and forests full of mushrooms and wonderful berries," Sveta continued.

"The only bad thing is the weather," Lyudmila admitted.

"Yes. Sometimes we have minus forty. Even minus fifty," Sveta said.

"Celsius," Lyudmila supplied.

The conversion between Celsius and Fahrenheit still confounded me, but these were temperatures I associated exclusively with cryogenic freezing.

"What about the summer?" I asked.

"Oh, in the summer we have midges."

"They are unbearable," Sveta moaned. "Clouds of them everywhere and they take big bites of your flesh. You put on a blouse and by the time you get to work it is streaked with blood."

"Well," I exclaimed heartily. "It certainly sounds worth a visit—"

"Alina!" Lyudmila interjected. "Why don't you take off your pants and drink with us?"

This request would have sounded much odder were it not for the fact that Sveta and Lyudmila themselves were wearing no pants and had made their way through most of a bottle of vodka during the course of our conversation. They weren't really bottomless, though, having torn the bedsheets off both Lyudmila's bed and mine and wrapped them around their waists. Seeing as how there were no bedsheets left, however, if I were to take off my pants, then I'd simply have . . . no pants.

"Thanks, guys," I said, "but I'm good."

"You will be much more comfortable!" Sveta said this with the kind of impatient tone normally reserved for a child who refuses to have a poopy diaper changed.

While I highly doubted that was true, what really worried me wasn't the taking off of the pants, but the drinking with Lyudmila, who had clearly gone pro. I might as well challenge Gary Kasparov to a game of chess or invite Bode Miller to hit the slopes with me.

"How about I make a beer run instead?" I suggested. Lyudmila and Sveta both agreed that a beer run did sound good, and as the only panted one among us, I was a perfect candidate for the job. I dashed off to the kiosk next door, and when I returned fifteen minutes later with a six-pack of Baltica, the television was on, Lyudmila was lying on her bed, and Sveta had a phone pressed to her ear.

"Shhh . . . my sunshine, my sweet . . ." she murmured. "What men? It is only myself and Lyudmila here. And a girl from America . . . Yes, America . . . Hm? . . . Don't be silly, that is only the television . . ."

"Alinachka," Lyudmila muttered. "Come. Take off your pants. Drink with us."

But Lyudmila had turned her bloodshot eyes to address the ashtray as she said this, so I didn't think to respond. Instead I lay down on my bed and considered how very odd it was that I did not feel scared, or uncomfortable, or even annoyed, trapped here in this room with two random Siberian woman, half nude and wholly wasted. I began to drift off, my mind making random associations. Sveta's sheet had slipped below her waist and I could see her thong riding up into Siberia. And then I was reminded of the Skoptsy, who had nothing inside their thongs, and their long years of Siberian exile. I thought about how, ultimately, the story of Siberia wasn't one of imprisonment, but one of survival. And how one man's exile was another man's freedom. I thought about the wallpaper, which in all Soviet-era hotels was strange and sad and faded and made me feel as though I were trapped inside a Sputnik that had been launched into outer space in 1971. And I thought about Nizhnevartovsk, its clouds of bloodthirsty midges hovering over shopping centers and sports arenas built with oil money. I thought about Josh. And then I took off my pants. And went to sleep.

GROWING INTO THE UNIVERSAL

know exactly what you're talking about," Konst said, lighting a cigarette. We were walking back home from dinner at Nine-D, our favorite Thai place in Carroll Gardens. It had just begun to snow. "For me it was a Lufthansa pilot."

"A pilot?" I wouldn't have expected Konst to be intimidated by a pilot, but I was curious enough to linger on the doorstep instead of leaving him there alone, to smoke in the cold and contemplate his hard, black lungs, like I usually did.

"I had to pick up a friend whose flight was scheduled to arrive at Tolmachevo at five a.m., and you know how that sucks."

I did know. Five a.m. was when the Moscow red-eye arrived in Novosibirsk, where Konst had lived and where my job occasionally sent me.

"Right. So that meant I had to get up at three in the morning and leave Akademgorodok by four. When I finally got to the airport, I caught a glimpse of myself in the mirror and Christ, did I look like shit. My eyes were bloodshot and what little hair I had left was sticking out like an insane clown's. But the most important thing was this: I just didn't give a flying fuck. It was late at night, so I looked at myself and figured . . . well, whatever."

Konst flicked his butt in the general direction of the Sunday trash pickup and we went upstairs. I turned on the electric teapot and Konst hung up his bowler hat and peacoat before sinking heavily onto a wooden folding chair. Though uncomfortable, the chair was goose down compared to the cheap foamcore couch from Target that shot an iron rod straight up your ass.

"So then the Lufthansa flight landed," Konst went on, "and the passengers came out, all these funksters just totally looking like shit. You know how when you're on an airplane all night, you come out covered in this kind of . . . film? And it just keeps absorbing the fluorescent light in the airport until you look like some kind of ghoul? That's what these people looked like. Then there's the fact that nobody is happy to be in Novosibirsk. Do you remember how the airport was back then? Like a shack in the field. So everyone is miserable."

"Okay, they are miserable and you look like shit . . ." I set down a couple of mugs and a box of Tropical Grapefruit Green Tea.

Konst examined the inside of his mug and, like mine, found a coffee stain at the bottom. He considered it for a moment, then tossed a teabag inside.

"Then suddenly the room temperature changes. Out comes the flight crew. The hostesses are first, and they're all very, very pretty. Very comfortable and worldly. But, you know, they were just a motorcade for what was to follow, for the arrival of the Übermensch." Konst paused a beat and gave me a meaningful look. "Finally, out comes the man himself, like something out of *Der Ring des Nibelungen*—"

"What's *Der Ring des Nibelungen*?" I interrupted. Konst always assumed a base level of competency in at least three foreign languages.

"It's an opera cycle by Wagner based on Norse mythology, and I'd say this pilot was straight out of the fourth opera, *Götterdämmerung*—Twilight of the Gods. First of all, he was taller than everyone else and he looked very fresh, very suntanned and well-coifed. And his teeth were like pearls. Okay, I sound like a girl now, but it's true. He was wearing a beautifully tailored uniform without a single wrinkle. But the most noticeable thing was that he projected this air of absolute authority, yet he wore it so easily." Konst broke off suddenly. "He needs a name. I think we should call him Helmut."

"Helmut." I nodded and poured the hot water.

"The thing is, somehow Helmut was not at all arrogant. Here he was at five in the morning, having flown a plane all night and just touched down in Siberia, and he was absolutely comfortable in both his environment and his own skin. I just looked at him and thought to myself, God, now this is intimidating. Here's a real pro. He gets up and he flies a fucking plane and people trust him with their lives. Helmut is a real person."

"And what about you?" I asked, hoping eagerly for the worst.

Konst blew on his tea, watching snow fall on the dark tangle of telephone wires outside the window.

"Me?" Konst asked, turning back to me, suddenly serious. "If he'd reached out to touch me, his hand would have gone straight through to the other side. Compared to Helmut, I am a nonperson. A beetle. A sad artifact."

To illustrate his point, Konst reached forward with one hand and pushed it straight through the chest of the imaginary Konst. We both stared at his hand, holding the heart of the apparition, the sad artifact who'd just pulled up a third chair to join us. There was a long minute when neither of us said anything.

"Okay," Konst said, knocking back the rest of his tea, "I've got the logline."

"What's a logline?" It was a night for new words.

"You know, the main idea—the summary of the script. Here it is: 'Quietly competent people in a real-world profession who are not flashy about it.'"

"I can see that," I said. "Nice." But I wasn't referring so much to the logline as to the fact that Konst had milked his neurosis enough to give Helmut a name and a logline. It felt good to know I wasn't alone in my insecurities. Only my Übermensch was not the female equivalent of Helmut, the woman I always saw breezing down an automated walkway at the airport, looking very Whole Foods, carrying nothing but a tasteful handbag, as I huffed along, jacket bunching up beneath the guitar on my back, struggling with a wheelie bag whose handle had just come off. I pictured her. She wakes up at some head-squeezing hour, eats half a grapefruit, and then heads off to a job where she does things that are interesting and useful while exhibiting unusually good posture. If I had to describe her in twelve words, I would say this: she has no pores and played field hockey in high school.

And yet, it wasn't the poreless, straight-backed female Helmut who stirred my deepest insecurities. My Übermensch was the opposite of Helmut.

My Übermensch was Britney, bitch.

It wasn't always that way. At first I hated Britney, as did everyone else I knew. Actually, before I hated her, I was just surprised at how she had managed to become such a big deal. I mean, was there anything more disingenuous than a teenage Britney Spears, falling out of a Catholic schoolgirl uniform while proclaiming, with pig-tailed innocence, that her loneliness was killing her? To my mind, a hot blond teenager seldom left unaccompanied by her synchronized dancing posse of also-hot teenagers would sooner be killed by a penny tossed from the top of the Willis Tower than die of loneliness. But these observations are all in retrospect for me. From my perch on the edge of things, it took a relatively long time to notice that Britney Spears had arrived. ". . . Baby One More Time" came and went and I was none the wiser. It was only in the spring of 2000, when "Oops! . . . I Did It Again" flattened the airways, that I woke up and smelled the Teen Spirit.

At the time, I was living in Texas, just out of art school, working for a small nonprofit organization. My hobby on the weekends was to drive out to remote towns with an old Hasselblad to photograph historically themed debutante balls, senior citizen beauty pageants, gatherings of the Texas secessionist movement, and things of that nature. I was a regular at the weekend turkey shoots out in Thrall and at a monthly African American rodeo in the rural hamlet of Plum, a place I couldn't find on any map. After work I liked to hang out at a trannie bar off the access road to Highway 290, which was famous for its drag competitions. I had heard the name Britney Spears but didn't know any of her songs, and if someone had asked me why I hadn't bothered to check out what looked to be the decade's biggest pop sensation, I would have proudly explained it was because Britney Spears was *normal*—she made corporate music for undiscriminating people—and I was *weird*. Then I would have excused myself to go shoot a cow-patty bingo contest out in Elgin.

I forget where I was when it happened. I could have been picking up some kitty litter at HEB, or raking leaves in our front yard, or having a Pap smear, or doing one of any number of commonplace things that inexorably lead to an encounter with a Britney Spears song, when I heard "Oops! . . . I Did It Again."

"This is the crappiest song ever," I complained to Josh back at home. And he agreed—it sucked. The video for "Oops!" features an eighteen-year-old Spears dancing in a suit so tight it looks as though she'd just been dipped in a piping-hot vat of melted red condoms. Its record-breaking sales made her the first female artist to have an album go platinum within one week of its release. But I knew zero of the 1.3 million people who bought "Oops! . . . I Did It Again" during that week in May of 2000, because I had surrounded myself with people who cared only about dark, obscure, and purposely difficult indie music. My friends and I listened to really small bands. The singers barely sang. Their voices wafted over to you through a galaxy of gauze run through a million effects pedals in reverse. The tempos were slow, sleep-inducing washes that cast you adrift in a pale sea of Mylanta, filling your mouth with a million, billion cotton balls. It was music that made you think, and even though the thoughts you thought were sad thoughts, you felt good thinking them, because this music was *deep*. And no one had ever heard it except you.

Before you are old enough to drive, the Massachusetts suburbs are typically a beautiful, lonely, and cold place to grow up. And as a lonely, cold, introverted child, the thing I most liked to do was sing at the top of my lungs, alone in the house while my parents were at work. The bathroom, of course, had the best acoustics, but warbling in the kitchen, which faced the street, offered at least some semblance of an audience—the mailman, a neighbor walking the dog, an airplane passing overhead on its way to Hanscom Air Force Base. My favorite venue, though, was the living room, where the windows overlooked a pond tucked into a droplet of forest. The view offered just the right dose of romantic inspiration for belting out pop ballads. I would serenade the pond, the indifferent box turtle sleeping on a log, the Canada geese serenely destroying the lawn, the ice hockey goalpost half sunk in the mire. I would treat them to Bonnie Tyler's "I Need a Hero" or John Waite's "Missing You" or Erasure's "A Little Respect," taking Whitney Houston down an octave, bringing Billy Idol up a notch, skipping the hard parts. This was the music I loved, that made me feel alive. I wasn't in Massachusetts anymore. I was onstage, buffeted by the white noise of an arena filled to capacity, flashbulbs illuminating the pitch like falling stars. Bringing the microphone to my lips, heart catching, I felt the weight of a million eyes. Somewhere behind me the canned music kicked on, the sound of a synthesizer desperately trying to be a violin. I was a superhero, a fruit roll-up made of equal parts Madonna, Cyndi Lauper, and Pat Benatar. When I tilted my head back and began to sing, it was with the power of a thousand microwaves exploding.

But over time I began to notice that eighties pop had strange physiological properties. After listening to it for a while you would start to feel . . . not so good. Hazy, restless, in need of fresh air. That's not to say that the music wasn't fun; it was. And a good single could still hit me like a speedball straight to the jugular. It's just that nothing could hide its fakeness. Eighties pop songs sounded like money—yet as cultural currency, they rarely lasted long. "That song is, like, *so* old," my friends and I would moan about some Duran Duran single released three weeks ago and still hovering at number seven on the Billboard charts. Like sunshine and sakitinis and Harry Potter books, eighties pop always left you wanting more. Another new song, another new voice, another perfect fix for a summer that always seemed to end too soon.

By the time I reached college, pop music made me want to eat a strychnine-and-tomato sandwich. It wasn't just a matter of taste anymore; I'd grown morally opposed to it. Not only to its big, tacky, and too often soulless sound, but also to the way it followed you everywhere all the time: the same ten songs hammering away on high rotation with Big Brother–like tenacity. And to the pop stars themselves, with their half inch of makeup and aggressive fashions, who didn't look like anyone I'd ever met. Even the normal-seeming ones, like John Cougar Mellencamp or Bruce Springsteen, loomed so much larger than life, with their perfectly round butts and carefully positioned bandanas, their jeans bluer than the bluest eye.

My horizons first started expanding in high school, when I started dating the kinds of geeky guys who knew everything about seventies punk or early American gospel, who clued me in to a whole world beyond the Billboard Hot 100. Then one day, on the way to my grandmother's apartment in Central Square, I bought an album, on cassette tape, from a busker who was playing on the subway platform. Her name was Mary Lou Lord, and a couple of times a week she would set up her Maxi Mouse battery-powered amp at Park Street station during the evening rush and sing sweet songs to tough guys from Southie waiting for the Braintree-bound Red Line. They would wait for her to finish and then yell down the platform, "Hey, Blondie, sing it again!" I remember sitting on the platform for more than an hour, missing train after train, before mustering up the courage to shuffle up to her guitar case and whisper, "How much?"

"Whatever you think it's worth," Mary Lou said. And I emptied my wallet and gave her everything I had—exactly ten dollars of babysitting money. The album was called *Real* and it was put out by a tiny independent record label in Santa Monica called Deep Music. I played it until the tape broke and then got a copy from another fan, my high school English teacher Molly. I played that copy until it broke too. Like Britney, Mary Lou mostly sang songs written by other people, but she found a way to make them her own. In her hushed, silvery voice, every word sounded so intimate, so *real*. Her music made me realize that you can synthesize a lot of things, you can Auto-Tune and add enough reverb to kill a horse, but you can't synthesize the feel of something homemade and handmade. With a fair amount of righteousness, I decided I didn't want to be the girl sitting at the end of the giant consumer conveyer belt with her mouth open anymore. I stopped listening to Top 40 radio. I stopped watching television. I finished high school, left the suburbs, and enrolled in art school.

It was only years later, during a long stint working in Siberia, a five-month stretch when my loneliness, so to speak, was killing me, that my resolve to ignore the mainstream finally began to melt—all because of Britney Spears. At the time, my work kept me traveling constantly. I spent many of my nights on the Trans-Siberian Express, going to sleep in one province and waking up the next morning hundreds of miles away. When I wasn't working, I would still go out exploring with my old Hasselblad, photographing midget circus performers, male strippers, a man in Tomsk who shared a one-bedroom apartment with eleven cats and a dead tree. It was as though, having run out of U.S. territory to be weird on, I had upped the ante by committing myself to documenting some of the most obscure denizens of one of the most obscure territories on Earth. But being weird full-time was hard work. It required eating lots of bad food. It necessitated the frequent use of squat toilets. Worst of all: it left me prone to unhealthy bouts of nostalgia. I was weird, but I was weak. The sight of a dusty Snickers bar in the window of a candy kiosk was enough to bring tears to my eyes. I missed America in all its mass-produced, culture-annihilating glory.

Throughout my epic tour of the world's least-heard-of places, there was only one constant, one never-varying soundtrack to even the most unlikely expedition, and that was Britney Spears's new hit, "Toxic." Or, to put it more accurately, the Swedish production duo Bloodshy & Avant's new hit, "Toxic." Actually, if you listen to the way the backup vocals swell suspiciously whenever any real singing is required, you start to wonder how much Britney really had to do with this song. But let's not quibble! The first time I heard it was in the overheated restaurant of the Hotel

Krasnoyarsk. There I was, having just returned to my table from the breakfast buffet with a bowl of cereal soaked in kefir and a mug of instant coffee, when I noticed the video blaring out of the television bolted to the wall in front of me.

The video begins with Britney on an airplane, playing the role of slutty stewardess. After serving some passengers their food using primarily her butt muscles, she lures an unsuspecting fat guy into the toilet for a make-out session, only to pull his face off and discover he is secretly a totally hot guy(!). Then Britney disappears—perhaps sucked through the airplane's waste-disposal system—only to emerge as a red-haired, leather-clad dominatrix, clutching Tyson Beckford's back as they zoom through Paris on a motorcycle. From there it's on to a spaceship designed by Ikea to pick up a green elixir and dance amid red laser beams in a tunnel. After some random footage from what appears to be somebody else's shampoo commercial, Britney transforms into a black-haired vixen and cleverly suction cups her way up the side of a building to break into the hot-guy-from-the-airplane's hotel room. Once inside, she is torn between the desire to make out with him and the desire to beat him up but eventually settles for just pouring the green elixir down his throat. That done, Britney runs away, jumping off the balcony, and lands right back in the airplane just in time to alert her passengers to stow their tray tables, using mainly her breasts. Intercut throughout the entire video is footage of Britney writhing around seductively wearing nothing but some glitter artfully applied with a Q-tip. The song won Spears her first and only Grammy. The video cost one million dollars.

From that moment on, "Toxic" followed me everywhere. And I mean everywhere; there was no escape, no hope of refuge even in the deepest, most godforsaken outposts of Siberia. On a bus rattling its way toward the village of Ongudai in distant Altai Republic, as "Toxic" assaulted a smattering of stone-faced

Babushkas, I remember getting angry. Rally yourselves, Comrades, I thought to myself. Fight the imperialist invaders! Doesn't Russia have its own cheesy blondes? Its own terrible pop music? But the Babushkas endured Britney without blinking. They had survived purges and the gulag, mass deprivation on an unimaginable scale. Britney was nothing—a mere hemorrhoid on the vast buttock of Russian suffering.

Somewhere, I pictured a marketing executive at Britney's label, Jive Records, standing over a digital map of the world studying mysterious clusters of pulsating LEDs, his finger traveling to a lone yellow blip, glowing in the dark penumbra of Russia's Arctic north like a french fry in outer space. Pressing an intercom button, he speaks:

"Jeeves? How is our market saturation in Siberia?"

"One hundred percent, sir. We have achieved maximum coverage."

"Is that right? Because I have some data here that shows there is a man in the Taymyr Autonomous Okrug, not far from the city of Dudinka, who has yet to hear the hit single 'Toxic.'"

"Some of these rural, ice-bound regions are extremely isolated, sir, well beyond the reach of the average radio signal."

"That's no excuse, Jeeves."

"Roger that, sir. I will contact our media buyer to increase radio presence in the Taymyr Autonomous Okrug immediately."

"See that you do, Jeeves. See that you do."

My father told me that back when he was a soldier in the Soviet army, the same two songs played all day long over the barrack's loudspeaker. The first was "Za Togo Parnya," about a soldier whose soul mate died during the war. The second, somewhat paradoxically, was a song written by a member of the indigenous Chukcha whose chorus went, "We will ride on deer into the dawn. You will see that the north is boundless and I am giving it to you." Papa's reaction to this aural onslaught followed the

Kübler-Ross model: his initial denial deepened into anger before culminating in eventual acceptance. And now that Siberia had become my personal Britney Spears boot camp, I too began to feel the effects of indoctrination. At first, the change was subtle. "Toxic" simply failed to annoy me anymore. And then soon enough—it could have been days or weeks or months later; I was somewhere, perhaps a salad bar in Kemerovo with plastic tongs suspended over the pickled herring—I found myself mouthing the words. A bit listlessly, true, but still. Then one day I simply woke up one morning with "Toxic" already thrumming through my thoughts, the start-up sound to my brain's computer.

Was "Toxic" a good song? I didn't know anymore. I was no longer fit to judge. There were more powerful forces at work here, engineering an allure that went far beyond the matter of the song's actual goodness. Millions of dollars had been spent on my conversion, the bandwidth of entire nations brought to heel. And some small part of me, I admit, was flattered by the attention. Britney Spears's music sounded like money, true, but it gave me a feeling that only money could buy.

Still, I couldn't help wondering where all this would lead. Every addiction starts with a harmless gesture—a puff, a taste, a sip, a snort. I would start off humming one Britney Spears song under my breath in Siberia and end up folding tube tops for a living at a Hot Topic in a mall on Staten Island, with nothing to look forward to but nights of scanning QVC for deals on gold-plated jewelry. I still couldn't shake the feeling that liking this kind of music *did* something to you, hollowed you out. What about that lost decade I spent lolling around on the carpet in my parents' living room, sucking on Capri Sun and mouthing the words along with Milli Vanilli? Even as my foot tapped along, I was filled with an infinite sadness. The sadness of every thirteen-year-old girl who loves to sing, who spends days staring into the flickering television screen at another singing girl who scarcely seems real. The thirteen-year-old girl who tries and tries to figure out a way to somehow get from her kitchen, with its humming appliances and sticky vinyl flooring and crushing normalcy, to that glittering, magical place. And then comes to the realization that it just can't be done.

It was Konst who first introduced me to the concept of "Growing into the Universal," a philosophy that was downright heroinlike in its ability to make my qualms about liking Britney go away. We met at a seminar in Novosibirsk, where Konst was working as an English translator, and even before we were introduced, I'd already taken notice of him in the halls. A heavyset man who bore more than a passing resemblance to Alfred Hitchcock, he favored bowler hats, chunky black glasses with clear lenses, and what appeared to be t-shirts from Brooklyn Industries, though of course that wasn't possible, was it? Over lunch one day, we found ourselves sharing a table in a cavernous hall, empty save for the enormous bouquet of fake flowers stapled to the wall, its dusty plastic vines trailing eerily all the way down to the floor.

"So what do you do back in New York?" Konst asked. I noticed that his English was impeccable, with only the faintest hint of accent.

"I work. I sing in a band too, and sometimes we play clubs in the city." I had long since put away my own Maxi Mouse street amp and upgraded to "real" venues, even though my songs were no less depressing and turgid.

"Really? What clubs?"

"Well, you probably wouldn't have heard of them . . ." because you live in what appears to be a total nonplace, you poor thing, I finished in my head.

"Try me."

"Well, our last show was at this place called Lit Lounge—"

"Oh, I know Lit. Cool place."

"How do you know Lit?"

"Nick Zinner likes to hang out there, right?"

"How do you *know* that?"

"Gothamist."

My forkful of fried beetroot froze halfway to my mouth. A man from the armpit of Siberia was telling me things I didn't know about a rock club across the river from my apartment in Hoboken.

The next afternoon, between sessions, Konst pulled me aside in the stairwell.

"Did you know that Matthew Barney is looking for interns?"

"How do you *know* that!?!"

"I read it on Gawker."

"What's Gawker?"

"What's Gawker? Are you fucking kidding me?" And with that, Konst pulled a flash drive out of his pocket and waggled it at me. "Hey, what do you say tonight my iTunes come over and have sex with your iTunes?"

We became friends and I learned that Konst was a recovering poet and aspiring screenwriter. He had grown up in Berdsk, a city not far from Novosibirsk, a place of anonymous plants making anonymous parts for anonymous weapons that distinguished itself mainly by virtue of not being Iskiteem, another city down the road, built around a cement factory that Berdsk dwellers had commemorated in rhyme:

> *On top there's dirt, below there's steam*
> *That's the city of Iskiteem!*

Konst was kicked out of high school in tenth grade, not long after *Lenin's Path*, the city newspaper, published an article declaring that all punk rockers were Nazis. Without a higher education, his options looked grim: a choice between either joining the army and risking getting sent to Afghanistan, or becoming a *fartsovshik*, selling jeans in the market. His father ended up finding him a job making coffins at a local factory instead. He spent his nights reading—Babel, Olesha, Nabokov—and attending the Berdsk School of Working Youth, a kind of reform school for Soviet losers. Then, one day, Konst took the entrance exams for Novosibirsk State University, one of the top schools in the country. To everyone's surprise, he passed.

Once in college, Konst became a full-fledged intellectual, able to discourse at length and in detail on any given subject: the Tartu school of semiotics, transformational grammar, the impact of *lubok* on Soviet poster art . . . But by the time I met him, this zeal for all things obscure, quirky, brainy, and difficult was something he was determined to beat out of himself. Konst called this quixotic mission "Growing into the Universal," a phrase he lifted from a book by Hans-Georg Gadamer called *Truth and Method*. One day, while perched on the Ikea sofa he and his girlfriend, Erika, had shipped to Siberia from Moscow, I asked Konst to explain exactly what "Growing into the Universal" was supposed to mean.

"It is the search for the mythological archetypes resting in the subconscious, the kind of iconography so primal that it appeals to everyone."

"Okay." Whatever that meant. "Like?"

"Like guns. Or girls. As Godard once said, all you need to make a movie is a girl and a gun. I might be wrong about this, but I am also considering that maybe helicopters are universal. And car chases—car chases are *definitely* universal. I can watch the same car-chase scenes over and over, even if it's a movie I've seen before. I get so caught up in the moment that I still find myself wondering what's going to happen next."

I wasn't sure whether I agreed with him on this point. Car chases made me tired. I found shoot-outs boring too, and could probably fall asleep watching four people sink to the bottom of a lake, trapped in a Toyota Camry, pounding on the windows and screaming as the cold water hit their privates. But Konst looked ready to dispatch all kinds of box-office statistics against me to prove his point, and besides, what did I know about the universal? My idea of a good movie was a documentary about the building of a hydroelectric dam across the Yenisey River.

There was really no mystery as to why Konst had come to embrace the universal and I had turned my back on it. While I spent the eighties watching ladies with impossible hairdos wrestle one another into swimming pools on *Knots Landing* and *Falcon Crest*, Konst was watching Soviet humanist dramas about real people living real lives and having real problems. Movies with titles like *Moscow Doesn't Believe in Tears* and *The Irony of Fate*.

"All this shit, this kitchen-sink realism—it was just suffocating. Always the same movie, over and over," he said, grimacing, waving his lit cigarette in the air like a traffic cop. "There'd be the longest takes. I remember sitting there and counting: twelve . . . thirteen . . . fourteen . . . just waiting for the shot to change. Then, all of a sudden in the late eighties, movies from the West became available, stuff like *Robocop* and *Terminator* and *Indiana Jones* and *Back to the Future*. And I'd look up at the screen and just think, Now shit is happening! See, that is what the universal is all about. It's about life quests! It's crude! It's robust! It's barbaric!"

"Yeah, but aren't a lot of big Hollywood movies just, like . . . bad?"

"Look, if you are a storyteller, don't be an elitist snob. Don't just cleverly mock the latest fad you saw on the subway. Do something that will *get* to people, whether they live in Vladivostok or

Tokyo. This is what I think: if you are into experimental shit, then go play the chain saw in a Stockhausen orchestra and just leave the rest of us alone."

Three years later, when Konst moved to L.A. to make it as a filmmaker, polite suggestions that he go the DIY route and start off, perhaps, by shooting a video on his cell phone and uploading it to YouTube would get blown off with a wave of the hand. His favorite movie was *The Bourne Identity* and he was working on writing his own unabashedly universal spy thriller.

"Forget it," Konst would tell people with a serene smile, "I am going straight into the ass of Hollywood."

Not long after I returned from Russia, Josh walked into our bedroom and discovered me sitting on the bed with my acoustic guitar, singing "Oops! . . . I Did It Again." I sang it slowly, mournfully, even a little angrily, as though Britney Spears and I were slowly dying of some incurable disease and this song was our last retort to an uncaring world. It was the song we had together, years ago, determined was crappy, and now, faced with justifying myself, I felt suddenly afraid. I wanted to repeat all the things Konst had told me, about how the four basic things in life were food, shelter, sex, and ritual, the latter of which included the cultural artifacts produced by Britney Spears. Then Josh would understand that by listening to "Oops! . . . I Did It Again" we were actually partaking, subconsciously, in rites and ceremonies that tapped into the mysteries of life itself. Britney *was* the Universal and the Universal was like fire, something that we could watch endlessly and still remain fascinated. But here was a man who had commuted to high school on a unicycle and spent the early part of his college years living in a tent in the woods. A man whose taste in books tended toward philosophical treatises in the original French or German, whose favorite films were subtitled, whose music collection was a veritable spice rack of human suffering . . .

"Hey," Josh said, taking a seat on the edge of the bed, "I really like that. Can you sing it again?"

I reached the pinnacle of my musical success after releasing an album covering the songs of Yanka Dyagileva, an obscure Soviet punk singer who had died young. I can still remember the stunned look on my parents' faces when I found them wandering the palatial lobby of Joe's Pub on the afternoon of the CD release show. It turned out that they'd been circling the building for half an hour, searching for a club that Papa diplomatically described as someplace "a little more cozy." The last time my parents saw me perform in New York, it was at Pianos, a small club on the Lower East Side. There had been exactly six people there: me, the two other singers on the bill, my parents, and Josh. And it hadn't felt cozy at all—it felt tense and scary and lonesome. I remember standing up to face my five-member audience and thinking: Wow, so this is what it feels like to fail in real time. I am in the process of failing right now—and now—and now.

But that was years ago and now we were here, at Joe's Pub, a posh dinner club tucked inside the landmark Joseph Papp Public Theater. I took my parents on a tour with Mama still eyeing me suspiciously, as though I were once again the sixteen-year-old prime suspect in the Case of the Watered-Down Vodka. When they returned to the box office that night, they were surprised to find a line stretching around the block; the show had sold out. All I wanted was to hold on to that feeling for a little while. The feeling of selling out a nice venue in Manhattan on a Friday night. The memory of my parents' being led off to a VIP area cordoned off by a plush velvet rope, looking more than a little slack-jawed. The discovery that the booker, who'd left Joe's Pub months ago to take a job at Lincoln Center, was waiting backstage

to congratulate me. This is just the beginning, I remember thinking to myself. But, in fact, it was more like the end. When I set off
on a nationwide tour to promote the album a few months later, I
found that outside of New York City, the thirst for harrowing
Soviet punk covers was not what I'd anticipated. In Philadelphia,
my band played to two people. In St. Louis, we had to cancel a
show at a club with a capacity of 250 because no one showed up.
By the time I reached North Carolina, I was wrung out, tired of
singing to no one, and tired of being weird. Basically, plain sick
of myself.

I was sitting at the bar of the Southern Rail, across the street
from the Carrboro Arts Center, where I was scheduled to play
that night, when I felt a hand gripping my wrist, interrupting my
fingers' regular commute to my mouth. It was Josh.

"Please!"

"What?"

"Please, please, please stop eating your fingers!"

"Why?" I asked, bewildered. The fact that chewing the dead
flesh off your hands was obviously disgusting apparently wasn't
reason enough.

"Because it is so unladylike. Will you just look at yourself?"

Ashamed, I'd looked down at my unmanicured, unpolished
nails buried in their scabby little divots. It was true: I looked like
I was trying to commit suicide by cheese grater.

Josh sat down at the bar.

"Maker's Mark, no ice," he said to the bartender. Then to
me, "What's wrong?"

"Britney Spears makes people happy, and I make people
sad," I blurted. The music the Swedes wrote for Britney had only
continued to grow on me; I had listened to little else on the long
drive east.

"I like your music. You're unique."

"Thanks." I said, draining my third vodka tonic. Britney has a fan base of millions, I thought to myself. I have a fan base of one.

"Sometimes I just wish I could make people happy too."

"I am going to give you an old Jewish parable. Are you listening? Okay, there was once this rabbi, let's call him Rabbi Shlomo. And he was just an ordinary rabbi, right? So one day he's talking to his friend and he's like, 'I'm just an ordinary rabbi. I don't do anything special or amazing. When I die, I know God will come to me and ask, "Why were you not Rabbi Akiva?" ' "

"Who's Rabbi Akiva?" I said.

"He was this totally amazing rabbi from the old times. Everyone knows about him, trust me. Anyway, so then his friend goes, 'Look, that's not what you should be worrying about. When you die, God won't come to you and say, "Why were you not Rabbi Akiva?" He'll say, "Why were you not Rabbi Shlomo?" ' "

I waited for Josh to finish, but apparently that was it.

By now the bartender had slipped away, his interest suddenly consumed by a stain on the far end of the bar. More likely he was just avoiding us, the toxic little cloud of misery I was generating. I knew Josh was right, but still . . . I didn't want to be stuck playing a chain saw in a Stockhausen orchestra. I didn't want to live alone with eleven cats and a dead tree, clinging to my barren rock of weirdness like the Little Prince drifting away on his lonely asteroid, waving at the night sky.

As I write this, Boy George recently completed a prison term for chaining a male escort to his wall. Michael Jackson is dead. Madonna is dating a twenty-three-year-old underwear model after getting over a nasty divorce. Tiffany lost twenty-eight pounds on *Celebrity Fit Club* and was a contender on *Hulk Hogan's Celebrity Championship Wrestling*. Bruce Hornsby and the Range—true to their name—now run a golf range near San Diego. Britney Spears is back on tour with a new album after having a mental breakdown, losing custody of her two children, and being placed under the legal conservatorship of her father.

As I write this, a thirteen-year-old girl somewhere in the world has decided that she wants to be the one on the other side of the screen, so she shoots a video of herself, uploads it to You-Tube, and instantly becomes a star.

THREE RANDOM FACEBOOK CHATS
WITH MEN I HAD ASSUMED
WERE FANS

10:20 a.m. Kleber
hello happy new year Alina
10:22 a.m. Alina
Hello Kleber! Happy New Year to you too!
10:23 a.m. Kleber
thank so fucking much, how are you doing?
10:23 a.m. Alina
fucking great! you?
10:25 a.m. Kleber
lol you killed me, i'm good too
10:25 a.m. Alina
Kleber?
10:26 a.m. Kleber
yes talk to me
10:26 a.m. Alina
Who are you?
10:28 a.m. Kleber
well i'm man who found ur profile interesting since u are with a
guitar
u must love music

10:31 a.m. Alina
Good detective work, Kleber! It is true that I love music. Have you made other friends using this method?
10:33 a.m. Kleber
hey we're not friends, we're just weird people chatting, anyway music is in my blood too
10:34 a.m. Kleber
i love music as i love chicken parmegana
10:39 a.m. Alina
It is good to clear the air and establish that we are just two weird people chatting about music and chicken parmegana. A bracing dose of honesty, that!
10:41 a.m. Alina
Are you a musician?
10:45 a.m. Kleber
yeah i'm looking to join a new band now cause my band just splitted
separated
i'm sad now
10:46 a.m. Alina
I'm sorry to hear that. It's sad when your band breaks up. It's like a boyfriend. Or a girlfriend.
10:49 a.m. Kleber
i know (i'm crying) even though i'm a man
thanx for understand me Alina
10:51 a.m. Alina
I know how it is, Kleber. I hope you feel better.

3:33 p.m. Nico
ciao Alina come stai
3:34 p.m. Alina
Bueno? Bono? Bien? I can't speak Italian.

3:35 p.m. Nico
ok that's not a problem
how are you doing
what's up
3:36 p.m. Alina
Well. The cat threw up on the blanket covering our sofa. And
then my husband sat on it.
3:37 p.m. Nico
i thought you was italian
3:38 p.m. Alina
sorry to disappoint you . . .
3:39 p.m. Nico
no it's not a problem i also like american people
3:39 p.m. Alina
that's good!
3:40 p.m. Nico
that's great
3:44 p.m. Alina
you're like Hillary Clinton
3:46 p.m. Nico
you're like Bill Clinton
3:47 p.m. Alina
This is getting a little surreal, Nico.

10:00 a.m. Arudra
hi
how do you do
10:01 a.m. Alina
I am doing good, Arudra! How about you?
10:01 a.m. Arudra
i am fine

10:01 a.m. Alina
You look a bit stern in your photo.

10:02 a.m. Arudra
what do you do as a profession

10:02 a.m. Alina
I am a singer. And you?

10:05 a.m. Arudra
i am a full time marketing consultant into film sales, yacht sales, private aviation services, olive oil, corporate training marketing etc
you are from which country

10:05 a.m. Alina
Wow. Yacht sales! I am from the US. Where are you from?

10:06 a.m. Arudra
are you looking at selling any music album in india

10:07 a.m. Alina
Sure. Why not? You could throw in a copy of my album with every yacht you sell as a special bonus!

10:07 a.m. Arudra
which segment of music you are into

10:08 a.m. Alina
folk rock

10:09 a.m. Arudra
i can sell your album if you give me a letter of authorisation of your company on company letter. it can be scanned and sent thru mail

10:10 a.m. Alina
I have no company. I am my own company. But why would you want to sell a folk rock album in India? Selling yachts, private aviation services and olive oil sounds way more exciting . . .

10:12 a.m. Arudra
okay then fine

YOU MUST GO AND WIN

When Josh and I moved to Brooklyn in May of 2009, two things began to die at once: my cat and my musical ambitions. The world was already deep into the economapocalypse, and a lot of arguably more important things were dying as well. Newsstands were lagoons of fear and sorrow: unemployment soaring, exotic species of bailout-resistant mortgages imploding daily, swine flu proving to be almost as bad as regular flu . . . Millions were suffering, and there I was, rummaging through the junk drawers of my own piddling problems. I felt guilty, but by then the drear was tinting everything. It had become a color, a season, a landscape you inhabit without ever noticing how the road bends to accommodate its slopes and valleys. It was hard to Hope for Change when the status quo felt like a Chevy Impala on the losing end of a monster truck match. Or when your cat was dying right in front of you.

The cat's name was Etsa, and by any standard, he was a terrible pet. He yowled incessantly, with great esophagus-ripping force. His hobbies were peeing on any stray piece of clothing that might have landed on the floor and shitting in shadowy crevices of the apartment. There were certain closets he would inhabit and defend with the ferocity of Robert E. Lee at the Second Battle of Bull Run. When we brought him home from the pound, a friend of ours suggested the name Etsa because the cat was Twinkie-colored, and Etsa, she explained, meant "sunbeam" in some Sri Lankan language. We took her advice, and, of course, since that day, every Sri Lankan native we've ever happened to meet has strenuously denied that Etsa means anything in either Sinhalese or Tamil. Now, whenever anyone inquired about the cat's name, we were forced to recount a story tedious for everyone and satisfying to none. Add to this that Josh named our other cat Zhuang-zi (after an ancient Chinese philosopher) and it is easy to understand why the vet's receptionist hated us.

"Er . . . Zoo hung zee? And . . . uh . . . Eeet za?" she'd call into the waiting area before a typical visit.

"That's *Zhuang-zi*," Josh would reply, with the intonation of a Jiangsu rice farmer, at which point the receptionist would begin stabbing us with her eyes. Fucking Yuppies, I could practically hear her hiss as we passed by on the way to the examination room.

Etsa was losing weight, but no one knew why. When we took him to the vet, she suggested there was nothing physically wrong with him, that our move had just stressed him out. Yes, no doubt, the move from a small, crappy sublet to a clean and spacious new apartment had been traumatic. But as far as I could tell, now that all the boxes were unpacked and the furniture put in place (things the cat didn't have to help with), Etsa was spending his day much as he always had: sleeping, shitting, blinking, and giving Zhuang-zi a rim job. Given that the cat already spent a good three quarters of the day unconscious, it was hard to figure out how else to help him chillax. Oriental foot massage? Detoxifying green tea baths? Aromatherapy? We brought the cat back to the vet, who did a round of blood tests. Everything came up normal.

We adjusted Etsa's diet, offering him a bonanza of Fancy Feast seafood and little salty treats that were probably made from repurposed bits of other cats. Nothing worked. The vet suggested X-rays. Our terrified pet was passed through the scanner, but still no explanation for his illness could be found. There was only one option left and that was invasive surgery, a biopsy.

Now, being a nonpurchaser of cat biopsies was something I happened to pride myself on. Let other people put a second mortgage on their home in order to fund Fluffy's dialysis, I'd think to myself. Last I heard, they were still giving away pets for free at the pound. This was a cat, after all, not a baby. And while some people confused their cat with a baby, I was determined not to be one of them. Maybe I felt defensive because it would be cool to have a baby but all I had was a lousy cat. But whatever, Josh and I were firm in our decision: no biopsy.

We brought Etsa home and he went about dying. He retched dramatically every day. He pooed on the sofa and peed on the bed. His weight kept dropping until I could see his bones poking through his fur. Some kids on my block set up a little donation booth to help fund their dog's surgery and I found myself putting a couple dollars into their fishbowl every day, rooting for their dog to live even though I kind of hated their dog. Etsa's meow changed; it grew soft and plaintive and sounded almost human. He was like Robert fucking De Niro with that meow. And the way he looked at me! Those eyes! Like giant satellite dishes beaming signals of infinite sadness from that shrunken little head. I couldn't stand it. I started to pray over the Russian Orthodox icon—a present from my priest, the Punk Monk— that hung in our living room. It was a prerevolutionary icon of Jesus, but during the Soviet era someone had scratched a thin white line into the paint to make it look like he was smoking a cigarette. The Punk Monk had told me I should cherish the icon all the more, for it had suffered, like Jesus had. It was a martyr icon. And I did find myself cherishing it more, but only because now Jesus reminded me of Kurt Cobain. After praying for guidance, I would kiss the icon, as per Orthodox tradition, always feeling a transgressive little thrill for lingering too long. Two weeks later, I made up my mind.

"Do you realize Etsa's biopsy costs the same as eleven days' rent?" I asked Josh. Now, from a financial perspective, all this really proved was that New York City rents were insane and that we should immediately pack off for some decaying rust-belt metropolis where homes sell for under twelve dollars. But Josh could see my point. We were already setting trash bags of money on fire every day anyway, just for the right to drink the Ritalin-enriched tap water New York City is known for.

"You're right," he said. "Let's do it."

When I wasn't busy massaging cat diarrhea out of my kitchen floor, I would contemplate my music career, which was also lying anemic in the corner. As with Etsa, everything looked good on paper, so it was hard to figure out the source of my trouble. I had finished recording a new album that was my best effort so far; my last album, which covered the music of an obscure Soviet punk singer and gave journalists a perfect excuse to finally use the word *magnitizdat*, had gotten lots of press; and, most auspiciously, I'd landed a book deal, which gave me a convenient platform to gloat about both of these things at length, a self-promotional clusterfuck my boss at the consulting firm where I worked part-time would call a "feedback loop." Still, there were some ducks missing from my row. Aside from a small but vocal core of depressed Jews, I didn't have much of a fan base. I also didn't have a label to put out my records anymore. Mine had gone bankrupt in the spring. One day I just received a message from one of the owners, Bryce, asking whether I'd be interested in buying back 1,456 copies of my first album and 43 copies of my second, all for the low, low price of $4,000. He was losing his storage space and if I wasn't interested in buying the albums, they'd end up in the dumpster. I didn't buy the albums. A few days later, the label's website went down and I haven't heard from the owners since.

Even so, I thought I'd found a way around these problems. While at South by Southwest in March, I'd met a manager who, impressed by my feedback loop, felt confident she could attract interest from a good label. We agreed to work together. I had heard stories about managers doing wonderful things for artists, so I decided to focus on writing my book and let nature take its course. But as the summer months passed, the only thing nature seemed to take was my cat. A few days after Etsa's biopsy, the vet called.

"We have a diagnosis," she said. "Etsa has gastrointestinal lymphosarcoma with additional inflammation in the stomach due to helicobacter bacteria. There were no cancer cells seen in the stomach specimen that was sent in, but I suspect it is there as well."

Etsa had cancer?

"You should probably come by now to pick up his medicine," the vet continued. "Let's start him on the prednisolone and the Leukeran right away. Then you can bring him back for a CBC recheck in a couple weeks."

When the phone rang, I was just about to leave for Connecticut to help a friend with his move. Instead, I drove to the vet to pick up the medicine and then rushed home to wrangle it into Etsa, still a frail, half-shaven wraith after his biopsy. By the time I got on the BQE, it was early in the afternoon and traffic was an angry, slow-moving mess. I inched along until the expressway gave way to the northeast corridor, and as I drove, I thought about Etsa. I had somehow convinced myself that so long as the vet couldn't find the source of his illness, he couldn't die. Like a cop insisting you can't have a murder without a body. But now it was done and those Latin words had put a boot to my throat. The cars jerked along. It was stop and go across all five lanes. I refused to cry. Remember, a cat is not a baby. I reached forward to change the Björk remixes that had been on auto repeat for the past two hours, suddenly feeling like I was trapped in the aural equivalent of a Stan Brakhage film and would rather eat my cell phone charger than listen to Björk for one more second. Reaching for the eject button, I felt it—a sickening jolt—and lurched, full-body, against the steering wheel. It was the semi right behind me. I'd been hit.

We both made our way over to the right lane, a maneuver that took five minutes and gave me plenty of time to reflect. The truck had rear-ended me, so legally, I wasn't at fault. But I knew my mind hadn't been on the road; I'd probably been stopping when I should have been going. I reached the shoulder and pulled over, the semi right behind me. A cat is not a baby, I thought, stepping out into the hot sun and rush of foul air, but a car isn't even a cat. The driver of the semi hopped down from the truck, which was big and expensive and bore the logo of a major corporation. He was a stocky Hispanic guy with a pitted face, not much taller than me and not much older either. As he got closer, I could see his face pulled taut with fear and concern. Maybe he was worried about his job. Maybe he had a family to support. And I'll never know what that man could read on my face, but when we reached each other, neither of us yelled. We didn't even talk. Instead, wordlessly, we hugged. Right there on the side of I-95, in full view of five stalled lanes of traffic, on a weedy, oil-soaked strip of land somewhere between Bridgeport and Fairfield, Connecticut.

"Look at my hands," the man said, holding them out in front of him, "they're still shaking."

"Everything's fine," I said. "Don't worry about it."

"I was so scared that maybe I hurt you—"

"You didn't hurt me. I'm sorry I scared you."

"Did you check the back of your car? I got my papers right here."

"I don't care about the back of my car. I park it on the street and it's all banged up anyway. Really. I'm okay. No papers."

The man asked me if I was sure and I said I was. We told each other to take care and I walked to my car and waited for the semi to pull back out onto the highway. Only after the truck had disappeared among the columns of cars, and I was sure the driver was out of sight, did I finally put my head down on the steering wheel and cry.

I needed something to help get my mind off things. It was a summer of endless rain, the future pregnant with the specter of cat funerals and imploded childhood dreams. I didn't want to just wait around anymore, getting slowly fucked by the fickle finger of fate. So when my friend Konst suggested we write a screenplay for an action thriller together—a project I was spectacularly unqualified for—I opened my mouth to say no and found myself saying yes instead.

It started back in April, when Konst was getting ready to move to L.A. and launch himself like a giant Russian enema into the ass of Hollywood. We were walking back from D'Amico's in Carroll Gardens, where we liked to go for coffee and spy on the locals.

"You know," said Konst, "I've been thinking that I'd really like to get in touch with my feminine side."

This was an interesting confession coming from a man who voiced conversational encouragement by yelling, "I've got my hand on my cock, bitch, keep going!" and disapproval by announcing, "Getting stiff over here, but not quite ready to tell you to turn around." Konst didn't want to get in touch with his feminine side; he wanted four-quadrant, big-box-office success. He wanted to get in touch with his third quadrant. And when he wasn't hanging around with me, he was probably slinging tapioca at the nursing home, stroking his geriatric side, or trying to avoid pederasty charges at the playground, in search of his inner child.

"Okay, shoot," I said. Konst liked ejaculation metaphors.

"Imagine that you are a girl. Okay?"

"Last I checked—"

"Right. But get this: you are *also* a wolverine—"

"This is some kind of horror movie?"

"No. A classic coming-of-age story. Because, see, you're *also* gay. Then one day you meet this German pinscher . . ."

When I got home, I created a Word file and saved it as "Idea Poo." Every time Konst said, "What if . . . ?" I double clicked on "Idea Poo" and wrote down whatever he said.

"What if . . . a tailor discovered that some thread he bought at a flea market had magical properties? We could call it *Fame Pants*!"

"What if . . . a ruthless stockbroker immersed in a prostitution-ring scandal suddenly falls in love with *a toy robot*?"

"What if . . . a woman born without any orifices overcomes hardship, while inspiring millions, to become a *paratrooper*?"

Then one day, Konst said, "What if . . ." followed by something that I actually found interesting. So I said, "And then what if . . . ?" To which Konst replied, "Then we could . . ." This routine continued after Konst moved to L.A. We'd spend hours on the phone running our characters through an aggregate of four different screenwriting frameworks, performing ever more complicated feats of computer-enabled psychoanalysis, until one day Konst exclaimed, "You know what, bitch? I think we're ready to stick it in and start pumping!"

It had to be the single most disgusting call to action that I'd ever heard in my life.

"Okay," I said. "As long as I can do the soundtrack."

Maybe that would save me. I hadn't been booking many shows lately. My manager was working on shopping my record and I was waiting for something to happen. That was my first mistake. Never wait for things to happen. When it became clear that nothing was going to happen, I knew exactly what to do. The answer was always the same: go DIY, take it to the people, jump in the van, tour, sing, tweet, blog. Announce yourself relentlessly to the world. My friend Roman summed it up best while visiting from Siberia a few years back. I remember it was morning and we were just mopping the last of the poached eggs from our plates when I started complaining about a show I had to play that night. I forget what my deal was. I bet it was a weekday, cold as shit outside, and I'd just have rather stayed home, curled up on the couch with Josh and some choice Netflix. Roman waited for me to finish and then looked me straight in the eye.

"Alina. This is a wrong attitude," he said. "You must go. And win."

You must go and win. Maybe it was the odd phrasing, the Russian accent with its lingering whiff of totalitarian decree. Or maybe it just suddenly hit me that I was complaining about taking a half-hour subway ride to play a club on the Lower East Side, to another musician, who had just traveled 5,694 miles, at great effort and expense, to do the same. Regardless, his words had the force of prophecy.

"You know . . . you're right, Roman." What was I complaining about? Why was I not taking advantage of America and all its freedoms, being all that I could be, carpeing my diem? I must go and win! Feeling born again, I spent the day in a small cloud of euphoria and then floated off to play a show at the Bowery Poetry Club that night to an audience of exactly two people.

Even so, all these years later, I knew Roman was still right. The only thing to do was plow on. Speak in the imperative. Go and win. But this time, I didn't want to go. I wanted to stay. If I went, then who would take care of Etsa? I was certain that, left in someone else's care, he would die. His medication was complicated. First there was the liver-flavored prednisolone chew tablet that he had to take twice a day, morning and night. Plus, after a recent spate of stomach trouble, the vet had me giving him 1 cc of liquid amoxicillin every twelve hours. There was a bag of nutrient-filled fluids in the closet to administer subcutaneously just in case he got too dehydrated, as he had that one night we had to take him to the animal hospital on Seventh Avenue. But worst of all was the Leukeran tablet. Etsa was a real thespian when it came to that Leukeran. He would hold it in his mouth for a good minute, staring me in the eye defiantly the whole time, only to spit it out as soon as I turned around. I finally succeeded in getting Etsa to swallow the pill through a combination of squeezing his little face, jamming a full syringe of water into the gap where his premolars used to be, and blowing on his nose, but I felt certain—and maybe this was excessive pride talking here—that no one else could ever master this delicate ballet. Yes, if I left, Etsa would surely die and then I would never forgive myself. So I canceled a show I had booked in San Francisco—only the second show I'd canceled since I started playing clubs six years before—and decided to stay in Brooklyn. Maybe, I figured, I could just stay and win.

Life was small and getting smaller. In an effort to make the most of my newfound domesticity, I got myself a plant. Feeling intrepid after it failed to die within three weeks, I bought another one. All of a sudden, I was like Brangelina let loose in a Romanian orphanage with those houseplants—no sooner had I amassed six than I started wanting a seventh. So in addition to Etsa's medication routine, I now had a plant watering and fertilization routine. I kept all the plants in the sunniest room, a room where the cats weren't allowed because they enjoyed throwing up on the couch in there. But with Etsa so weak, Zhuang-zi no longer had anyone to play with, so I took to letting him trot along after me when I went to water the plants. It was during one of these visits, while perched on the forbidden couch, that Zhuang-zi challenged our new desert palm, Ziggy, to a duel. Though he aquitted himself admirably, Zhuang-zi was no match for the plant. With his dozens of long, scissored leaves, Ziggy made quick work of him. The next morning we discovered Zhuang-zi sitting on his red pillow in the kitchen, his eyes swollen shut and oozing pus. He had managed to scratch both of his corneas. That afternoon, the vet installed a large plastic cone around his head and prescribed an antibiotic ointment to be squeezed delicately onto the surface of each eyeball three times a day. This treatment was to be followed by a warm compress over each eye. When Josh and I arrived home, we set the cat carrier down, opened the door, and stared at each other numbly. There was a sound— *shhlp-thuck, shhlp-thuck*—and we looked down to find Zhuang-zi, his peripheral vision gone, banging into the table leg again and again.

So now we had Zhuang-zi, miserable in his cone, eyes crusted over, unable to eat or drink without assistance, and Etsa, looking like some victim of cat Auschwitz. Friends would come over, survey the feline wreckage scattered across the living room, and gasp, "What happened?!?"

"Nothing!" I'd pip, desperate to preserve some semblance of normalcy. "Some cheese and crackers?"

Given that now I was almost completely tethered to my apartment and couldn't travel very far, I dedicated whatever tiny crevices of time not spent at work or applying cat compresses to exploring the neighborhood. My neighborhood, I soon learned, is a great place to go if you want neon lights installed underneath your truck or need to do some laundry at three in the morning. It is also a great place to die. There were five funeral homes within six blocks of my apartment, and the Green-Wood Cemetery was just a ten-minute walk away. As a rule, cemeteries are great places to remind yourself that things could always be worse. Maybe this is why I found myself hanging out at the Green-Wood more and more. One morning, after feeding Etsa his Leukeran and prednisolone and treating each of Zhuang-zi's eyeballs with a translucent dollop of oxytetracycline hydrochloride, I decided to head over there for a stroll. On my way, I passed a group of twelve-year-olds on the corner trying to light a cigar, and a man sitting outside a Laundromat yelling, "Tell your ma I ain't gonna pay for it," over and over into a cell phone. I loved my neighborhood. When I reached the Green-Wood gates, I just stood there for a moment, narcotized by the blasting sunshine and the endless fields of the dead, with their unspeakable, unsolvable problems. Then I skipped off to Battle Hill.

The best tombs were up on Battle Hill, and whenever I spotted one I liked, I would try the doors. Then, if I could make out an inscription on the back wall—sad, timeless things like "Until the

Day Breaks and the Shadows Flee Away"—I'd jot it down in a little notebook. After writing down inscriptions and thinking melancholy, poetical thoughts, I would drift around the graves feeling very Emily Dickinson–ish, and head off to the chapel, where, if no one else was around, I could enjoy the great acoustics and sing for a while. This was my routine. But today I skipped the chapel and stuck with the tombs. What would it be like, I wondered, to have a little patch of land here? My own marble-fronted mausoleum with a cushy stone bench, some framed photos, maybe an iPod on the windowsill for inspiration?

On my way out, I approached the guard. "Excuse me," I said, "but is your sales office open? My grandfather is terminally ill and I'm looking to buy a grave." I couldn't believe the terrible things winging out of my mouth. Both of my grandfathers were already dead.

The guard told me that the sales office wasn't open on weekends but we got into a conversation, and I quickly learned that buying real estate in the Green-Wood was no different from buying a condo in Manhattan. Battle Hill, it turned out, was the equivalent of Beverly Hills; you paid more for proximity to famous people, even in death. A hundred years ago, the guard told me, you could get a plot in the Green-Wood for just twenty-five dollars; today a prime spot could cost you well over quarter of a million. Wow, I thought, eyeing the graves with new and hungry eyes. Even at $300,000 for 756 square feet, a mausoleum was still a relative steal compared to most studios, especially considering the Green-Wood's proximity to the R and N lines. Not to mention the view of Manhattan, twenty-four-hour concierge, and ample parking!

I chatted pleasantly with the guard for a long time, but eventually had to pry myself away to go meet my friend Ben back at my apartment. He was making an experimental film about the

Italian Futurists and had cast Etsa in the role of Franz Joseph I, ruler of Austria-Hungary from 1848 until 1916. I had worried about whether Etsa was really up to it, given his condition, but it turned out that all Franz Joseph was required to do was sit on a blanket while eating a piece of cheese and wearing a gold paper crown on his head. Ben would film Etsa eating the cheese and I would stand by with an ostrich feather just in case his attention started to drift off camera. For this, I was to earn a credit as "Special Assistant to Etsa the Cat." I had no idea what any of this was supposed to mean, but since confusion was the bread and butter of the experimental film industry, I imagined that Ben must be doing quite well for himself. As I walked home, I couldn't stop thinking about the dead—savvy real estate investors all of them—snug within their quietly appreciating assets. I was jealous. It must be nice not having to worry about things. There weren't many upsides to being dead, but a sense of lasting stability was, perhaps, one of them. I think that might have been when the idea came to me. The idea of committing indie-rock suicide.

On the one hand I knew that as soon as I stopped making that leap of faith, stopped believing (without much in the way of bill-paying evidence) that if I just worked hard enough, wrote good songs, and toured endlessly, I could someday quit the day job that sent me—true, only occasionally, but still—to staff the company trade show booth in chilly, cavernous hangars, next to other exhibitors selling modular, climate-controlled mortuary facilities, or squishy, keychain-sized testicular self-evaluation models, it was never going to happen.

On the other hand, it was never going to happen.

And as soon as that thought settled in my mind, I knew the game was up. What if I didn't go and win? What if I stayed and lost? For the first time, instead of filling me with dread, the idea filled me with a strange euphoria. No more traveling long distances to play half-empty clubs. No more worrying about what to do with this new album. I could opt out of all those tedious discussions about how to creatively package music so that people would actually pay for it again. (I will bake my CD into a stack of pancakes! I will embed MP3s in toilet paper! My next album will take the form of a nasal inhalant!)

My own thirty-fifth birthday was only two weeks away. Too early for a midlife crisis, perhaps, but not too late to consider the trade-offs I'd made. For the past five years I'd worked as an assistant at a consulting firm, a job whose one shining virtue was it allowed me to arrange my schedule around touring. Though grateful for the flexibility, half the time I wasn't even sure what exactly my job was. Whenever people asked, "What do you do?" my eyes would invariably drop to trace an incredibly interesting pattern on the floor I'd only just discovered. Eventually I gave up on even trying to answer the question, choosing to just parrot it back instead.

"Yes . . ." I would echo hopelessly. "What *do* I do?"

My friend Gabe tried to help me once. "Something with PowerPoint?" he'd suggested.

Something with PowerPoint. This was actually a pretty good answer, I had thought with growing excitement. Most of my work days were so consumed with slide formatting that sometimes I regretted having studied international development when a master's in Microsoft Office, with a concentration in PowerPoint, would have served me much better. Gabe was right. But now another voice whispered: Wait! A hundred years from now, did I want a girl to go skipping through the Green-Wood Cemetery, heart full of song, only to pause at my tricked-out mausoleum, try the door, and discover the words *Something with PowerPoint* inscribed on the back wall in peeling gothic letters?

I recalled all the stories I'd heard about the artists who didn't make it, whose fates didn't turn on a dime one day, retroactively bronzing every early failure with the glow of inevitability. And after a glass of wine or three, I had to admit, there were some other things I might like to do in this life that weren't compatible with spending months each year driving from bar to bar, frittering away the hours before soundcheck with some drunk guy insisting that a goblin was staring at his pants.

And there was something else. Around this time, a music blogger included me in a top-ten list of his favorite female singers. He sent me the link, and when I looked at it, I immediately sensed that my name was out of place. The other singers on the list were all on well-established labels. Their songs were featured in movies, on television, in iPod commercials. They provided the background music for high-end hipster shopping. In some way, I realized, their success was defined by comparison with singers like me—if the list were reorganized in food-chain order, I would be the plankton. Then I noticed something else: of the other nine singers on the list, seven were older than I was and only one—a singer whose husband was also a musician, and who could tour as a family—had a child. Now, maybe the rest of these obviously successful, ambitious, and talented women just weren't the maternal types, but I suspected something else might be at play here. My guess was that this, too, was a matter of trade-offs.

It was true that I didn't belong on that list, I thought to myself. I hoped in more ways than one.

The problem was *how* to quit. After all, America does not like a quitter. In a broader sense, I knew that my exit from the music scene would cause not a ripple. At worst, my core fan base of depressed Jews might find themselves a little more depressed. But in this, I felt like I was practically doing them a favor. No, for my own sake I needed a way to explain the sudden change of heart, a beautiful, glass-half-full way to spin this, like, "Don't think of me as a failed musician when *really* I'm a successful cat nurse!" After all, Etsa had turned a corner, hadn't he? The closets were once again redolent of cat pee, and lately he'd begun standing outside our bedroom door in the mornings again, serenading us with his bloodless screams. All the gains I'd found so elusive in other spheres of life were now satisfyingly felt here, in pounds and ounces.

Still, it would be good to have a non-cat-based explanation handy for quitting indie rock, and I actually figured this would be easy, for I'd long been in the habit of collecting quotes that made losing look like winning. It started back in high school, after a sadistic English teacher forced us to read *Middlemarch* and I found myself jotting down George Eliot's last memorable description of the long-suffering heroine, Dorothea, on an index card and taping it to my closet door: "For the growing good of the world is partly dependent on unhistoric acts; and that things are not so ill with you and me as they might have been, is half owing to the number who lived faithfully a hidden life, and rest in unvisited tombs." At the time I had no idea why I felt the need to write this down. Perhaps, instinctively, I sensed a missed marketing opportunity, a spokeswoman for those of us who just wanted to be let down easy, the weak-hearted seeking a good excuse not to try. Where were our how-not-to books and unmotivational speakers? Then, a little while later when reading *Franny and Zooey*, I stumbled across another gem and automatically reached for a pen: ". . . just because I like applause and people to rave about me, doesn't make it right. I'm ashamed of it. I'm sick of it. I'm sick of not having the courage to be an absolute nobody. I'm sick of myself and everybody else that wants to make some kind of a splash."

A new vision was forming in my young, impressionable mind. It was a lofty goal, but with hard work and persistence, I might just get there. To be an absolute nobody and rest in an unvisited tomb. I could go live in this appealing alternative universe, a place with no SAT prep classes or varsity sports, where the heroes were the ones carrying out unhistoric acts in the welcome shade of obscurity, like contestants in some noble race to the bottom. But I didn't turn up the best quote until college, when I read a short, heartbreaking essay by Tillie Olsen called "I Stand Here Ironing," in which she writes of her oldest daughter: "She has much to her and probably little will come of it . . . Let her be. So all that is in her will not bloom—but in how many does it? There is still enough left to live by."

Was there ever such a beautiful ode to lost potential? It became the crown jewel in my canon of loser literature. And recalling it now, my heart soared. So all that is in me will not bloom! Let me be! There is still enough to live by! So true. I had to tell someone, but who to tell? I knew that Josh wouldn't have much faith in my change of heart. He would remind me of the other times I'd cried wolf. Worse, he would tell me to "remember the rabbit."

It was a few years back, while traveling in Turkey together, that we'd visited the fortune-telling rabbit. The rabbit had its own outdoor stand just outside the Hagia Sophia mosque. When we arrived, he was sitting on a wooden board littered with folded-up wads of paper, blinking into the sun, nose working furiously. We handed some money to a Kurdish man—apparently the rabbit's manager—and he asked for my name. Then he nudged the rabbit, who promptly scampered across the board and picked up one of the fortunes in his mouth. The man handed us the fortune. We unwrapped it, only to confront a line of indecipherable squiggles.

"It's written in Kurdish," the man explained, then took the fortune back, offering to read it to us.

"If you smile the world, it smile you back," the man read. "If you frown, it frown you back. Your mistake is to frown."

Josh was overjoyed. He pointed at the rabbit, who'd turned his butt to us and was now contentedly munching on a carrot. "That rabbit," he said, "is right about everything."

From then on, whenever I started bitching and moaning about my prospects in life, threatening to quit this or that endeavor, swearing up and down to finally become "a real person," Josh would just peacefully wait out the torrent of words, and then, with Dalai Lama–like simplicity, intone, "You smile the world? It smile you back."

In the end, I arranged to meet my friend Sarah for dinner.

Sarah was a publicist at a well-known rock PR firm, but our connection had nothing to do with music. We had met a few years back when I randomly answered an ad on Craigslist and ended up subletting a room in her Williamsburg loft for a couple months while I was shopping my first album to labels. During this time I managed to catch fleas and hurt my back so badly that Josh had to wheel me out of her building on a furniture dolly. Sarah, meanwhile, spent that time making famous rock stars even more famous. Somehow we stayed friends.

We met up at Republic in Union Square and took a seat on the patio outside. Sarah told me about her fabulous rock clientele, their hot new albums, and the limitless revenue streams fanning out before them like glistening rows of watermelon ripe for the harvest, while I sat quietly, all that was in me not blooming. Finally, she paused before bringing a forkful of pad thai up to her mouth to ask me how things were going with my music, a question she had asked many times before.

"I'm quitting!" I practically yelled.

"What!" Sarah said. "Why?"

I wanted to say something beautiful or bitter or wise, like

Salinger or Eliot or Olsen, but instead I yammered something about the nebulous state of the music industry and about feeling generally demoralized and awash in doubt. I barely managed to stop myself before getting into the ravaging effects of feline gastrointestinal lymphosarcoma.

"Don't be silly," Sarah said, plowing into her pad thai with some measure of relief. "We just need to find you a new manager, someone who can help get your album out."

"No, no, no," I said. "This is it. I'm done. I'm quitting. But don't worry, it's not some kind of tragedy. I'm happy about it. Can't you tell I'm happy?"

Sarah eyed me uncertainly.

"Besides," I continued breathlessly, "I have a new plan. I'm working on a screenplay with Konst. An action thriller!" As soon as the words were out of my mouth, I regretted them. I sounded like a down-and-out character from some Jim Jarmusch film, the broad with a cigarette voice, desperate for reinvention.

"Well," she began, "I guess if you're happy . . ." but suddenly her eyes skated past me and lit up. She grabbed my arm. "Oh my God! Look, it's the Hulk!"

I turned around and, indeed, there was a very beefy man, his chest spanning about six versts, lumbering down the street.

"Do you realize what a rare sighting this is? I haven't seen the Hulk in, like, a year!" Sarah whisper-hissed.

I had never seen the Hulk before, or even heard of him for that matter, but my wonder was soon eclipsed by another attraction not five steps away: a man with a black-and-white tabby cat balanced perfectly on top of his head. I shit you not. I hadn't visited Union Square in a while, and in my absence it seemed to have transformed into one of those tiny cars vomiting out an endless stream of clowns onto the sidewalk, each more improbably bizarre than the last.

Sarah's eyes flicked to the Cat Man, then back down to her plate. "Oh. *That* guy. I see him all the time out on Sixth Avenue."

I was surprised at how little interest Sarah showed in the Cat Man. But then again, she'd grown up on Staten Island, not a one-Starbucks town like mine. I was still hick enough to be dazzled. The Cat Man stepped into the doorway between Republic and the Heartland Brewery. He stood on the little spit of asphalt separating two islands of patio diners, making sure he had everyone's attention. Then he carefully set the cat down on the ground.

"Nick! Hey, Nick!" the Cat Man yelled. "Get upstairs." At this, the cat pivoted wildly to make an impressive vertical ascent up the Cat Man's body, scrambling right up the side of his face to regain his perch on top of the man's head.

"Jesus! Did you see that?" I said to Sarah.

"Uh-huh," Sarah replied, not looking up.

I gave the Cat Man two dollars, and Sarah and I went back to our conversation. I was hoping we would return to the topic of my quitting music, hoping, somehow, that Sarah would beg me to reconsider. I was suddenly feeling not so sure of myself. Maybe it would be better, more noble and pure and self-effacing, to simply accept my status as plankton, recognizing the important role plankton plays in nourishing the stature of the guppies, dolphins, and blue whales of the indie-rock world? But the parade of Seuss-like characters down Union Square West had apparently wiped Sarah's memory slate clean. Now she was talking about a client she had to accompany to an important photo shoot the next day for a major fashion magazine, and the difficulties of hitting the promotional sweet spot where rock-and-roll rebel meets high fashionista. It *was* tricky, I commiserated. I mean, modeling sunglasses for Diesel is one thing and donning de la Renta for *Vogue* quite another, but that middle ground?

Pure *Lord of the Flies* wilderness. Well, such were the vicissitudes of life at the top, I guess. We paid our bill and made our way up Sixteenth Street.

"And the thing is, I don't even know what to wear myself. I mean, it's not *my* fashion shoot, but still, I have to make a good impression, you know?" Sarah was saying. We had taken a left on Sixth Avenue and I was about to reply, when I noticed the Cat Man a block away, heading toward us.

"Look! There he is again," I said.

"See?" said Sarah. "I told you. Not rare."

When we were within spitting distance, the Cat Man stopped and gave us an expectant look. Nick peered down hungrily at us as well, his front paws delicately balanced on the brim of the man's baseball cap.

"I just gave you two dollars, remember?" I said. "Back in Union Square."

"Yeah?" the Cat Man said, the word marinating in his thick New York brogue. "An ya just boughtchaself a little piece in 'eavan wid dat."

We kept walking down Sixth but the Cat Man stood there, calling after us.

"It's allabout karma!" he hollered. "Give a little, get a little. Everything comes back around, ya know."

"It's hard to take a man seriously when he has a cat on his head," I remarked.

"Right." Sarah snorted. "These 'gems.'" She laughed. I wanted to laugh too, but something stopped me. After all, how different were we, the Cat Man and I, when I could practically feel the weight of my own cat on my head? Make that two. I considered all the cats—and remembered the rabbit.

We stopped at the mouth of the subway to say goodbye.

"Well," Sarah said. "God. It is kind of sad, you quitting music. My mind's kinda . . . blown."

"Yes," I agreed eagerly, hoping for more. "It is sad. Really sad. Right?"

"Yes," she sighed, then suddenly brightened. "But, hey, like you said, you're happy. That's all that matters." She gave me a quick squeeze and disappeared into the tunnel, handbag swinging.

And then I turned in the opposite direction and ran. I could have sworn I heard my train coming.

ACKNOWLEDGMENTS

I owe a great deal to the early readers of this book, foremost my parents, and especially my mother, Inna Simone, who not only accepted my debatable version of events with incredible grace and good humor, but whose comments always clarified any weak spots with chilling accuracy. Andrei Konst, thank you for founding the world's tiniest and most elite writing group with me, for your relentless cheerleading, and for being such a unique and irrepressible force of nature. Sarah Lindemann-Komarova and Vanya Komarov: your infectious enthusiasm made finishing each chapter all the more worthwhile.

Thanks also to the Massachusetts Mafia: Eugene Mirman— you are right, I will always be in the midst of a nervous break- down, but luckily you will always be around to provide unlicensed therapy; Amanda "Fucking" Palmer (www.amandapalmer.net, twitter.com/amandapalmer, myspace.com/amandapalmer) for your friendship and for setting me on the path to absurdity at a young age; and to the indescribably fantastic Ben Coonley, I hope we continue to troll the galleries of Chelsea together until we are both old and grumpy. Er, grumpier.

Onward with this dogged crusade of thanks! Thanks to Punk Monk and Brother Scott Phillips for spiritual enlightenment, or in Scott's case, simply lightenment, and to Sarah Avrin—everyone needs at least one happy, well-adjusted person in their life, and you are mine. Similarly, everyone needs one unrelentingly bitter friend in her life, and in my case that would be Dan Moller, who endured many questionable earlier drafts of this work. I lay wreaths of gratitude at the feet of my bandmates, Shawn Setaro, Conrad Doucette, Chris Barrey, and Satish (with special thanks to drummer John Lynch for making my years in North Carolina so Carrborific), to Bob Gourley for tech support and Sheila Kenny for fabulousness support.

To Joshua, my stealth editor, thank you for applying your considerable intellect to debating the relative funniness of "Power Ass" versus "Ass Power," and for enduring life with Etsa the cat for more than a decade now. You have the patience of Job.

Speaking of "patience of Job," enormous thanks to the long-suffering Eugenie Cha. At first I felt bad about how your youth was being squandered, chained to a desk at Farrar, Straus and Giroux, making sure my manuscript was in tip-top shape. But now that I see the final result, I cannot help but cheer! Just kidding (sort of). Also, many thanks to Kathy Daneman at FSG and to this book's illustrator, Vladimir Zimakov.

And finally, this book would not exist were it not for Eric Chinski, who wrote to me out of the blue one day, yammering something incomprehensible about the Owl of Minerva, and inquiring about my writing. Thank you for cajoling this book into being, Chinski, and for being so incredibly sweet and supportive. You are the kind of guy who will always give his cupcake to the girl stuck in the elevator, and I am lucky you found me, luckier still to count you as a friend.